Amphibians and Reptiles

Species • Habitat • Behaviour

Contents

INTRODUCTION

SALAMANDERS   8

FROGS AND TOADS   16

SNAKES   32

Amphibians and reptiles

Amphibians are found all over the world, represented by more than 4,400 species. Salamanders, newts, frogs and toads are all amphibians. Although amphibians and reptiles are frequently confused, they are easy to tell apart: reptiles always have scales, and amphibians never do.

There are more than 6,000 species of reptiles. Like amphibians, they are cold blooded, with their largest populations found in tropical and subtropical regions. Their body temperature is dependent on the temperature of the environment and overall tends to be lower than that of mammals and birds.

Amphibian skin has no scales, hair or feathers. With the exception of caecilians, all amphibians have skin that requires a certain level of moisture. This is why so many species live only in the tropical rain forest. Those that live in cold or dry zones must at least have the opportunity to store up moisture and heat. This is most important for the amphibian's sense of touch, which is governed by a network of nerve endings located throughout the skin. In cooler regions, amphibians hibernate during the winter months.

With few exceptions, amphibians need water in order to reproduce, as their eggs are laid and their young develop in water. The gradual, incremental transformation from egg to adult is called metamorphosis. Fish-like amphibian larvae begin life breathing in water through internal or external gills, ending up as land animals breathing air with lungs.

Amphibians tend to be solitary creatures occupying the same territory their entire lives. Males and

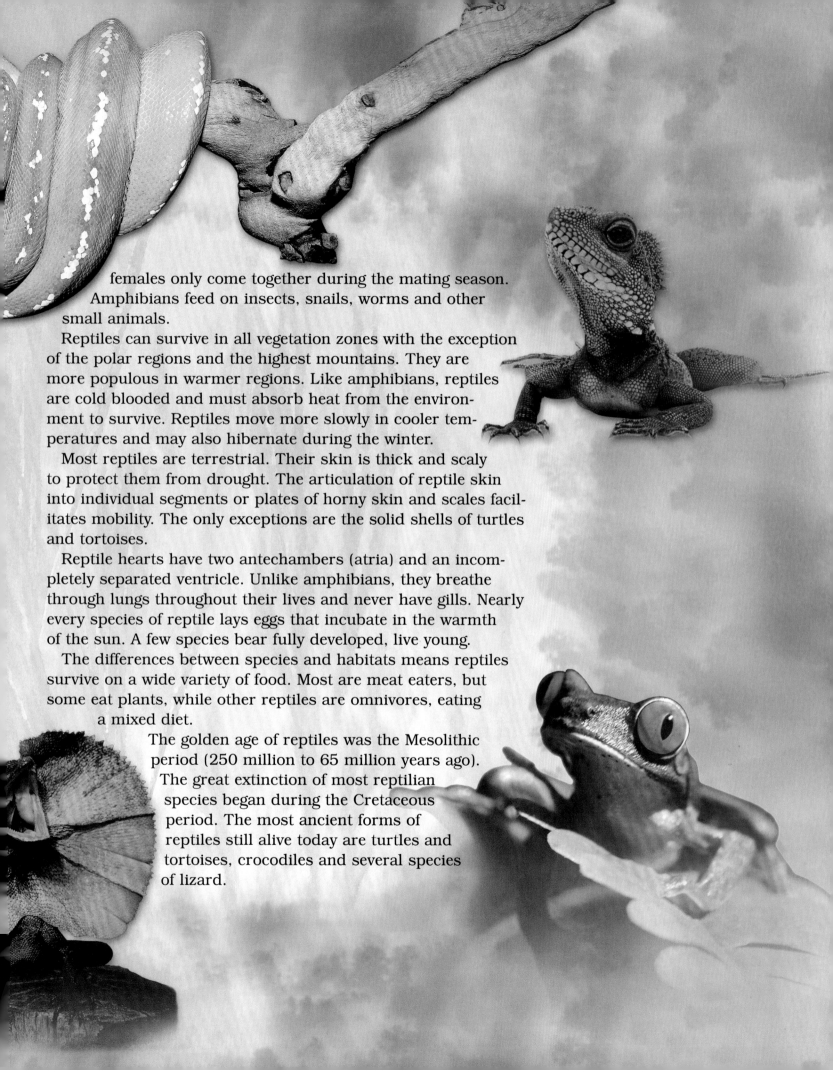

females only come together during the mating season. Amphibians feed on insects, snails, worms and other small animals.

Reptiles can survive in all vegetation zones with the exception of the polar regions and the highest mountains. They are more populous in warmer regions. Like amphibians, reptiles are cold blooded and must absorb heat from the environment to survive. Reptiles move more slowly in cooler temperatures and may also hibernate during the winter.

Most reptiles are terrestrial. Their skin is thick and scaly to protect them from drought. The articulation of reptile skin into individual segments or plates of horny skin and scales facilitates mobility. The only exceptions are the solid shells of turtles and tortoises.

Reptile hearts have two antechambers (atria) and an incompletely separated ventricle. Unlike amphibians, they breathe through lungs throughout their lives and never have gills. Nearly every species of reptile lays eggs that incubate in the warmth of the sun. A few species bear fully developed, live young.

The differences between species and habitats means reptiles survive on a wide variety of food. Most are meat eaters, but some eat plants, while other reptiles are omnivores, eating a mixed diet.

The golden age of reptiles was the Mesolithic period (250 million to 65 million years ago). The great extinction of most reptilian species began during the Cretaceous period. The most ancient forms of reptiles still alive today are turtles and tortoises, crocodiles and several species of lizard.

CHAPTER 1

Salamanders

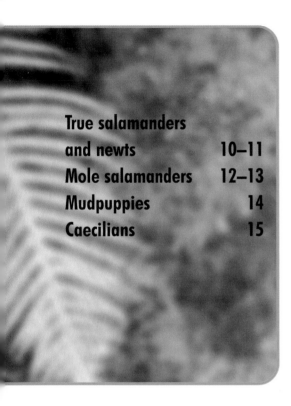

Represented by over 300 different species, salamanders are one of the most important groups of amphibians. Most occupy temperate zones in the northern hemisphere. Nearly all live in water or very moist habitats, some of them under rocks or in caves. Most salamanders spend the day in hiding, emerging only at night to hunt worms, spiders, snails or small invertebrates. Like most amphibians, they hibernate during the winter or periods of drought.

Salamanders have an elongated, reptile-like body, a long tail and four short legs. The front feet have three to four toes and the rear feet have two to five toes. Sometimes these are missing altogether. Most salamander skin is dark with lighter spots or stripes. Glands in the skin exude a sticky slime. Salamanders frequently shed their skin, but never all at once, like lizards or snakes, and therefore much less noticeably. If a salamander loses a limb, it can easily grow a new one.

Like all amphibians, salamanders reproduce in water. The male salamander deposits a bundle of sperm on a rock or stick. The female takes the sperm up into her body through the anal opening, and fertilization takes place internally. The female salamander will return to the same pond or stream to lay her eggs. Newts use sticky slime to anchor their eggs to a rock or aquatic plant. Like all amphibians, salamander young will not leave the water until they have developed lungs for breathing air.

The salamander family is made up of true salamanders and newts, mole salamanders and mudpuppies.

Also described in this chapter are the caecilians (*gymnophiona*), a unique group of amphibians with atypical characteristics.

Fire salamander

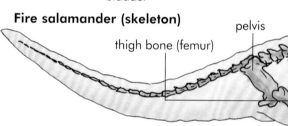

The family of true salamanders and newts (*Salamandridae*) includes fire salamanders, alpine salamanders and most varieties of newts. Forty-two different species live in the temperate regions of Europe, North America, Asia and northwest Africa.

Physical characteristics include an elongated, somewhat plump body with a tail that is round in section. Four limbs have four well-developed toes on the front legs and five on the rear legs. Skin is usually smooth and rich in glands that exude a sticky slime.

Nearly all true salamanders and newts begin life in water, whether as eggs or live-born larvae. Young salamanders and newts begin as gill breathers and end up as adults with fully developed lungs. Fertilization is always internal, with the sperm drawn into the female body via specialized sex organs.

The Alpine salamander (*Salamandra atra*) is unique in mating away from water. Females give birth to two completely developed live young without laying eggs.

Outside of the mating period and metamorphosis from larva to adult,

most newts – such as the pond newt, mountain newt and crested newt – do not spend much time in water. Most will also overwinter entirely on land.

In contrast to most newts, fully aquatic newts are slenderer and more elongated with a paddle tail better suited to swimming. Males often develop a crest along their back.

Unique among amphibians, newts not only regenerate lost limbs, but can also regrow their internal and sensory organs. A newt that loses an eye can grow a new one.

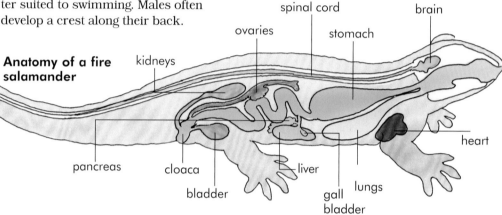

Anatomy of a fire salamander

ovaries · spinal cord · brain · kidneys · stomach · heart · pancreas · cloaca · liver · bladder · gall bladder · lungs

Fire salamander (skeleton)

thigh bone (femur) · pelvis

Fire salamanders

Fire salamanders (*Salamandra salamandra*) are true salamanders that live in deciduous forests, rolling hills and low mountain ranges throughout central and southern Europe and north-western Africa. Most can be found in moist environments near a water source.

Fire salamanders can grow to 20 cm long, with varieties in the Balkans reaching over 30 cm in length. A fire salamander's most distinctive feature by far is its skin colour. Characteristically vivid yellow spots over a dark background cover its entire body.

The skin of a fire salamander exudes sticky slime that irritates the eyes, nose and mouth of any attackers

Cross-section of the skin of an amphibian, for example, a salamander.

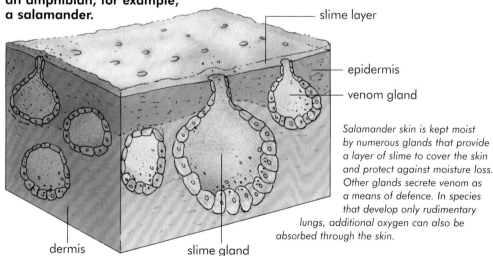

slime layer · epidermis · venom gland · dermis · slime gland

Salamander skin is kept moist by numerous glands that provide a layer of slime to cover the skin and protect against moisture loss. Other glands secrete venom as a means of defence. In species that develop only rudimentary lungs, additional oxygen can also be absorbed through the skin.

Fire salamander
(Salamandra salamandra)

Hellbenders

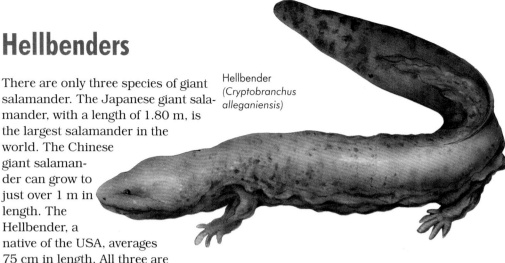

Hellbender
(Cryptobranchus
alleganiensis)

and can, in some circumstances, be deadly.

Food sources include snails, worms and all kinds of insects. Fire salamanders hunt primarily at night.

Fire salamanders usually mate on land soon after waking from their winter hibernation. The male carries the female off on his back and deposits his sperm packet on the ground nearby. The female slides over the packet repeatedly, taking the sperm into her body. Fertilization is entirely internal.

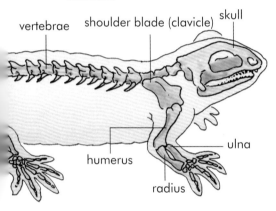

vertebrae   shoulder blade (clavicle)   skull

humerus

radius

ulna

Following an incubation period of up to 10 months, as many as 50 live young will be born in water. They will breath through external gills for the first two to three months while their lungs develop, after which they can live on land.

There are only three species of giant salamander. The Japanese giant salamander, with a length of 1.80 m, is the largest salamander in the world. The Chinese giant salamander can grow to just over 1 m in length. The Hellbender, a native of the USA, averages 75 cm in length. All three are among the most ancient of all salamander species. They spend their entire lives in water.

Hellbenders (*Cryptobranchus allaganiensis*) are native to eastern and Midwest America states with a range from New York to Kansas. They have a flat head and a flat paddle tail that acts as a rudder. Wrinkled skin covers its entire body.

Hellbenders spend the day hiding between rocks under water. At night, aided by an exceptional sense of

The mountain newt

The mountain newt (*Triturus alpestris*), also known as the Alpine newt, lives in the hills and valleys of Europe, as well as in mountain ranges below the altitude of 3,000 m. They are about 11 cm long with a grey upper body, orange-red lower body, and a transitional spotted zone in between. The throat area is also often covered in dark spots.

smell, and an even better sense of touch, Hellbenders leave their lair to hunt snails, worms, and small crustaceans. With eyes located far apart on both sides of its head, a Hellbender has no binocular vision. It relies on other senses to judge distance from prey.

To reproduce, male Hellbenders dig a burrow well protected by rocks and stones. The female lays strings of up to 500 eggs in the nest hole, which the male fertilizes with sperm. The male will guard the nest for the next eight to ten weeks until the larva hatch.

Mountain newts eat insect larvae, snails, earthworms and spiders. If they live near lakes they also feast on small crustaceans.

Female mountain newts lay their eggs on water plants between the months of February and May. The larvae develop slowly and may not leave the lake or stream until autumn.

Other newt species include the pond newt, crested newt and striped newt.

Male mountain newt
(Triturus alpestris) with
its mating season colouration

11

Mole salamanders

Mole salamanders (*Ambystomatidae*) are found throughout North America, from Canada to Mexico. The name comes from their distinctive, mole-like incisors and their tendency to burrow under the earth.

The majority of mole salamanders are terrestrial, spending their time above or below ground. A few species live in or near water their entire lives.

Mole salamanders have elongated bodies and long tails with the lines of the rib cage clearly visible through the skin. Most are between 8 and 30 cm long. Skin colour and markings vary widely. Males and females are nearly identical, with the male's tail just slightly longer. The skull is very broad and the eyes are very small. Adults are air breathers with well-developed lungs. Mole salamanders eat worms, small invertebrates and insects.

During the mating season, mole salamanders travel to nearby mud puddles or small, seasonal ponds. This is why mating usually takes place only after heavy rainfall in late winter or early spring. How they know exactly where to go is unknown. Mating typically takes place under the protection of darkness. After a series of complex mating rituals, the male deposits sperm bundles on the ground, which the female draws up into her body. Fertilization is internal, and eggs are laid in the same puddle or pond, usually at night.

Larvae hatch with feathery external gills and a strong, rudder-like tail for swimming through the water. If they survive to adulthood, they will lose both the gills and the flat end of their tail.

Mole salamanders are unusual in that they can reproduce before leaving their larval stage. The scientific term for this species survival behaviour is *neoteny*.

Among the best-known mole salamanders are the marbled salamander (*Ambystoma opacum*), the spotted salamander (*Ambystoma maculatum*), the Pacific giant salamander (*Dicamptodon ensatus*) and the Axolotl (*Ambystoma mexicanum*).

Axolotl

The Axolotl (*Ambystoma mexicanum*) is only found in Mexico, primarily in the area around Lake Xochimlico near Mexico City. The Aztecs gave them the name, which means "water monsters" in their language.

The Axolotl is about 30 cm long. In its natural habitat the skin is dark, but if raised in captivity most Axolotl will be albino, with pale or white skin. Axolotls have a dorsal crest that runs along their entire body down to the tip of the tail and prominent, feathery gills. Although they have legs and feet, their limbs are not particularly well developed or strong.

Axolotls spend their entire lives in water, never developing beyond what in other amphibians would be considered a larval stage. Despite this genetically programmed lack of development, they still reproduce. Mating progresses more or less the same as with other mole salamander species and could, theoretically, lead to Axolotls that fully metamorphose and develop lungs to live on land.

The number of Axolotls in existence today is greatly reduced due to the loss of their natural habitat through urban development and pollution. They are also easy prey for predatory fish. Last but not least, many are trapped for the illegal pet trade.

Pacific giant salamander

The Pacific giant salamander (*Dicamptodon ensatus*) is found on the north-western coast of the Pacific Ocean.

These giants grow up to 30 cm long, with stout bodies and a massive tail. The Pacific giant salamander's body is marbled with dark markings and a light coloured underside. Its limbs are notably massive and well

Pacific giant salamander
(*Dicamptodon ensatus*)

Marbled salamander
(Ambystoma opacum)

Axolotl (Ambystoma mexicanum)

developed. The broad, flattened head swells noticeably at the temples. Its eyes project slightly and are a shiny, light golden colour.

In contrast to most other species of salamander, the Pacific giant salamander has vocal cords. It uses these to make a barking or croaking sound when it feels threatened.

The Pacific giant salamander is at home on moist woodland floors, as well as along rivers, creeks and mountain lakes. It eats snails and other small creatures, and is not afraid to go after snakes if it is hungry.

Reproduction takes place in the spring, when the female lays up to 100 eggs on branches underwater. Unique among salamanders, each egg is attached to the branch by means of a small spur. Females guard the eggs until the larvae hatch, already bearing powerful tails and small gill slits. They live as predators in the region's cold lakes and icy mountain creeks. Their main food is insects and the larvae of other amphibian species, including tadpoles. When they are 10 to 15 cm long, most metamorphose into adults and leave the water. While most Pacific giant salamanders are sexually mature by their second year on land, some will never leave the water because they have failed to develop lungs. They will instead continue in the larval stage until they are 20–25 cm long, after which they will be able to reproduce without having developed full adult anatomy (*neoteny*).

Marbled salamanders

Marbled salamanders (*Ambystoma opacum*) can be found in a wide variety of habitats. They live in swampy areas, but also on dry, forested hillsides. Like most salamanders, they are never far from

a river or pond. They range from New England to northern Florida, and as far west as Texas.

Marbled salamanders are black with silvery grey markings that are somewhat lighter on females than males. They are small, just 10–12 cm long. The marbled salamander has the most powerful tail of all the mole salamanders and, unlike other species in this group, does not lay its eggs in water.

Their diet consists primarily of worms and slugs that they hunt by night. During the day they hide under rocks and twigs.

Unlike other salamanders, nearly all of which breed in spring, marbled salamanders mate during autumn. Fertilization is internal. Eggs are laid in shallow holes dug into the ground. Approximately 100–300 eggs will be laid at a time, watched over by the female until they hatch. This protects the eggs from being eaten by insects or other salamanders.

When it rains, the nest hole fills up rapidly and the larvae hatch all at once. If it does not rain, the eggs laid during the autumn can remain in the earth until the following year without any damage. Full-grown larvae are about 7 cm long.

Mudpuppies

Common mudpuppy
(*Necturus maculosus*)

The family to which mudpuppies belong (*Proteidae*) includes six species, all occupying fresh water habitats in Europe and North America. Mudpuppies live entirely in water, and are sometimes referred to as aquatic salamanders. Like several other kinds of salamander, mudpuppies spend their entire lives in a larval stage without ever developing lungs.

Mudpuppies have an elongated body and a distinctive, fish-like snout. They can grow to 30 cm in length. Their legs are vestigial and poorly developed. Their skulls are cartilaginous instead of bony, with no bone in the upper jaw to support teeth. Instead, mudpuppies have two rows of teeth (inner and outer) within the lower jaw. Mudpuppies have tiny, yet functional eyes. In some species these are completely covered by skin.

Mudpuppies, unlike other salamanders that remain in a larval stage, have very small, nearly useless lungs in addition to their external feathered gills. Varieties of mudpuppy include the common mudpuppy and cave salamanders, which are nearly blind. Mudpuppies can survive on land for short periods of time.

Common mudpuppy

The common mudpuppy (*Necturus maculosus*) lives in the eastern USA and Canada in clear, sandy creeks, as well as muddy canals and ditches

They can grow to 40 cm, making them the largest, as well as the most widespread, species of *Proteidae*. Their skin is grey to dark brown with irregular black spots and a tan or light grey underbelly. The distinctive snout slopes to a point. The skull is notably egg-shaped. The neck area is distinguished by a vividly red bundle of external gills. The common mud-

puppy's protruding eyes are extremely small and entirely lidless. Its tail is flat and rudder-like. The four underdeveloped limbs have four to five toes.

Common mudpuppies spend most of their time submerged in the mud of a riverbed, or lying under rocks. In the late spring, females, carrying eggs that were fertilized in the autumn, lay their 60 or so eggs in the water or between the roots of an old tree stump. After one to two months, the eggs hatch and 2-mm long larvae emerge.

Common mudpuppies are genetically very similar to cave salamanders. Both are nocturnal and live on a similar diet of insect larvae, small aquatic crustaceans and worms.

Cave salamanders

Nearly all the species of mudpuppy live exclusively in the lakes and rivers of North America. One exception is the cave salamander (*Proteus anguineus*), found primarily in the limestone caverns of Italy and Croatia.

Like the common mudpuppy, cave salamanders have bright red bundles

of external gills that they retain their entire lives. They never develop lungs.

Cave salamanders can grow to 25–30 cm in length, with a cylindrical body and nearly colourless skin. Its limbs are completely underdeveloped. The eyes have evolved to adapt to its environment of near-total darkness in subterranean caves

and their rivers and lakes. Shrunken skin grows over the eye sockets, leaving the cave salamander effectively blind.

Cave salamanders eat small crustaceans, snails and aquatic worms.

Female cave salamanders lay up to 70 eggs beneath a rock. Males and females watch over the eggs until they hatch. The larvae emerge after about two months.

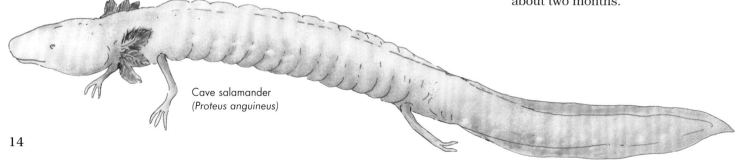

Cave salamander
(*Proteus anguineus*)

14

Caecilians

Caecilians (*Gymnophiona*) live in both tropical and subtropical regions. They tend to live in the uppermost layer of fertile, well-drained soils. Only one variety is entirely aquatic.

The body of a caecilian is distinctly ringed, with the number of rings equal to the number of its vertebrae. Caecilians are the only amphibian that sometimes has scales, formed from calcite deposits on the surface of the skin.

With their rings and complete lack of limbs, caecilians often resemble oversized earthworms. The smaller varieties grow to 20 cm in length, with the large ones as long as 60 cm. When on the surface, they move along the ground like snakes, but

Ringed caecilian
(*Siphonops annulatus*)

spend most of their time underground hunting prey.

Caecilian eyes and hearing organs are underdeveloped, but their sense of smell is extremely sharp. Adults also have a pair of mobile tentacles (feelers) between their eyes to help them hunt a wide variety of insects and worms.

Not much is known about how caecilians reproduce. Some species lay eggs and have gilled larvae that develop in water. Others develop almost entirely inside the female's body while still in the egg. When the eggs hatch, the young caecilians, still with gills, line up in the oviduct and, and, through its walls, take in nourishment directly through their skin. By the time they are ready to leave their mother's body, they have already developed lungs and exchanged

their thin larval skin for the scaly skin of an adult caecilian.

When on the surface, caecilians are frequently the prey of snakes and birds. The aquatic varieties are food for fish, turtles and frogs.

Caecilian species include the common caecilian (*Caeciliidae*), fish caecilians (*Ichthyophiidae*) and aquatic caecilians (*Typhlonectidae*).

Ringed Caecilian

The ringed caecilian (*Siphonops annulatus*) is abundant in the South American countries of Ecuador, Brazil, Peru and Argentina, where it grows to around 35 cm. Its body is proportionately thicker than the other caecilians and, also atypically, it has no scales. Ringed caecilians are

overwhelmingly subterranean, but have nonetheless retained a pair of very small, functional eyes.

Ringed caecilians survive mainly on worms hunted underground, but are also known to attack ant nests. Although it is known that they lay eggs, it is not entirely clear how the eggs and larvae develop.

São Tomé caecilian

The São Tomé caecilian (*Schistometopum thomense*) is variety of common caecilian. It lives underground only in the forests of West Africa.

São Tomé caecilians can grow to 30 cm. Their bodies are brightly coloured orange-brown. They dig under the forest floor to hunt for their diet of worms, insects and other invertebrates. The eggs of these caecilians hatch inside the body of the mother, who gives birth to almost fully developed young.

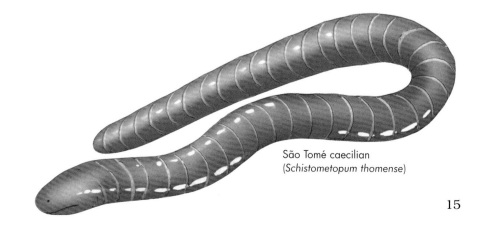

São Tomé caecilian
(*Schistometopum thomense*)

CHAPTER 2

Frogs and Toads

With over 2,600 species, frogs and toads (*Anura*) are one of the largest groups of amphibians. They can be found all over the world with the exception of very cold and very dry regions. The greatest variety of frogs and toads are found in Africa.

Frogs and toads have a distinctive body type with a plump body, short neck and a very large, rigid head characterized by oversized, protruding eyes. Their front legs are proportionately short with four toes. Their rear legs are long and powerful with five toes, often webbed. As such, frogs don't really swim. Instead, they propel themselves forward by jumping, whether in water or on land. They hunt insects and other small animal prey.

Most frogs and toads live primarily on land, but are rarely far from water. Nearly every species of frog and toad returns to water during the mating season to lay eggs. This can lead to massive migrations of hundreds or thousands of these amphibians to the pond or stream of their birth every spring. Most frog and toad species spend the winter in large groups wherever conditions are best for hibernation.

Male frogs and toads have a vocal sac to amplify the croaking sounds made during the spring to attract females. This "frog chorus" can be heard from far away. Females lay their gelatinous eggs in strings or clumps, always in the water. Upon hatching, the larvae, called tadpoles, swim with an oversized, powerful tail, breathe through gills and feed primarily on water plants. During metamorphosis, the tail disappears almost entirely as the tadpoles grow legs, a broader mouth and lungs. As adults, frogs and toads are well adapted to life on land.

True Frogs

True frogs (*Ranidae*) are found all over the world, but primarily in Africa, Europe and Asia, with almost no species known in South America and Australia. True frogs have highly specialized leg musculature and are exceptional jumpers and swimmers.

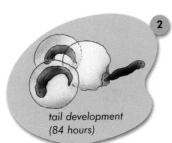

fertilized eggs

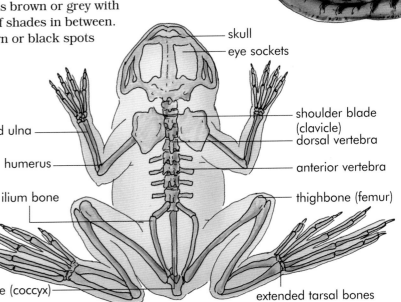

tail development
(84 hours)

external gill development
(6 days)

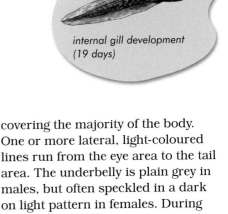

internal gill development
(19 days)

While all frogs and toads spend the mating season and metamorphosis in swamps, ponds and creeks, true frogs pass most of the summer months on land, returning to water in the fall. As the weather cools, they dig themselves deep into the mud and hibernate under the ice. In tropical regions, they dig hibernation burrows during the dry season.

One of the most representative species of true frog is the European water frog, also known as the "edible" frog (*Rana esculenta*). It hibernates deep in the mud during the winter. In the spring, the males emerge croaking loudly to attract females. Two white vocal act as amplifiers, each about the size of a cherry, located on either side of the throat. Often, several males pursue a single female, who may lay up to 10,000 eggs at a time in a slimy mass. In most true frogs, the process of metamorphosis from egg to adulthood takes around four months.

The largest species of frog, at nearly 40 cm, is the Goliath frog (*Gigantorana goliath*). It is native to West Africa where it lives in rivers with deep, freshwater pools where it can hide at the slightest sign of danger.

Grass frog

The grass frog (*Rana temporaria*) is native to most of the European continent, absent only from Portugal, southern France, Spain, Greece and Italy. Its distribution extends as far east as Asia.

The grass frog is one of the many "brown frogs" found around the world. Its skin is brown or grey with a wide variety of shades in between. Most have brown or black spots covering the majority of the body. One or more lateral, light-coloured lines run from the eye area to the tail area. The underbelly is plain grey in males, but often speckled in a dark on light pattern in females. During the mating season the males have a bluish cast to their skin. This comes from reserves of lymph built up during the long winter hibernation. In contrast, females have more vivid, intense colouration during the mating season. Grass frogs average 10 cm in length with a plump, sack-like body, broad head and short, blunt snout.

During the summer, grass frogs frequent areas with low vegetation, such as meadows, agricultural fields, gardens or old growth forest clearings.

They can also survive in mountain regions. Adult grass frogs are largely nocturnal hunters. They eat

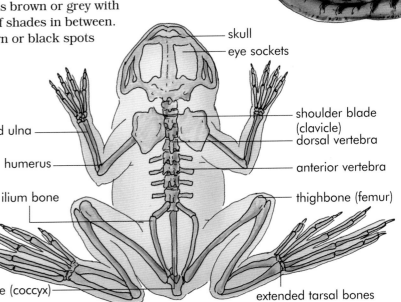

Grass frog (skeleton)

skull
eye sockets
radius and ulna
humerus
ilium bone
toes
tailbone (coccyx)
shoulder blade (clavicle)
dorsal vertebra
anterior vertebra
thighbone (femur)
extended tarsal bones of the foot

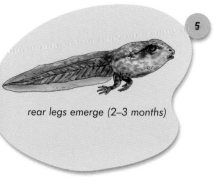

rear legs emerge (2–3 months)

front legs emerge (3 months)

fully developed adult grass frog

reabsorption of the tail marks the end of metamorphosis (4 months)

Frog and toad metamorphosis

insects, spiders, crustaceans, worms and snails.

In the fall, grass frogs migrate to their winter quarters, which are usually burrows dug underwater into mud. They can also overwinter in drainage ditches or caves. The frogs will not eat at all during hibernation, surviving on the fat reservoirs in their bodies.

In mid-February, grass frogs emerge from hibernation and begin their migration to their nesting sites. These are usually still, calm bodies of water, but ditches, puddles or even rain-filled tire tracks will suffice. The males "sing", often all at once in chorus, in order to attract females. The grass frog has a dull, muffled croak that, individually, is not very loud. The grass frog chorus takes place around noon and at dusk. A male will often locate and mount

Grass frog (Rana temporaria)

a suitable female during the migration, before arriving at the nesting place, covering her cloaca with his body. A male that has attached himself to a female will kick away other males that try to approach her.

Eggs can be laid wherever there is a still body of water. Females deposit slime-covered clumps of eggs that are immediately fertilized by the male. Eggs will continue to be laid until the clump is fist-sized, after which the female leaves the water, while the male stays behind. Males remain in the water, perhaps to protect the eggs, for several weeks before returning to land.

Eggs hatch after 10 to 14 days, although cold weather can delay hatching for as long as a month. Since grass frogs lay their eggs earlier in the season than other competing species, their tadpoles feast on the eggs laid by other frogs. This keeps the population of other frogs in check. By June or July, grass frog tadpoles have fully developed into adults. They leave the water when they are 10–15 mm in length. Adult size is dependent on environmental influences including weather, habitat and size of the population. Grass frogs are able to reproduce when they are three years old.

Grass frog (anatomy)

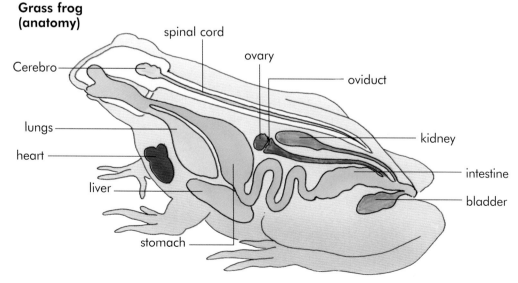

spinal cord

ovary

Cerebro

oviduct

lungs

kidney

heart

intestine

liver

bladder

stomach

South African bullfrog (*Pyxicephalus adspersus*)

Bullfrogs

Bullfrogs (*Rana catesbeiana*) live in and around the waters of eastern North America. With its broad, massive body up to 20 cm in length, the bullfrog is the largest frog on the continent. All bullfrogs belong to the group of true frogs and toads.

Unlike other species of frog, bullfrogs lack anatomically discrete slime glands. Instead, slime is excreted from a distinctive fold in the skin (the dorsolateral fold), which reaches from the top of the eye, around an oversized tympanic membrane, and ends where the foreleg attaches to the body. The tympanic membrane is as large or, particularly in males, even larger than the eye. A bullfrog's vocal sacs are all internal. Its characteristic deep, loud vocalization inflates the throat region and can be heard from very far off. It resembles the bellow of an ox or bull, which is likely how the bullfrog received its name.

The bullfrog is olive-brown or green and can be spotted or plain with a light coloured underbelly. Its legs are frequently speckled. The webbing between its rear feet is particularly extensive and can reach up to the tip of the fourth toes.

During the day, bullfrogs can be found sunning themselves on the shores of ponds and swamps. The slightest disturbance sends them leaping away. They are nocturnal hunters, feeding on insects, fish and smaller frogs. They are also known to eat baby birds and snakes. Although several bullfrogs might occupy the same pond, they are usually solitary even during the mating season, a time when other frog species tend to congregate and migrate in large groups.

Female bullfrogs can lay as many as 20,000 eggs, which they drag to the surface of the water and attach to plants. The tadpoles hatch after only five days, but it can take five years for them to metamorphose into adults. In southern regions, metamorphosis may take just one year. This is still much longer than for other frog species.

Bullfrogs are champion jumpers. Many can cover ten times their body length in one leap.

In addition to the North American bullfrog, there are other bullfrog species around the world. The South African bullfrog (*Pyxicephalus adspersus*) lives in the savannah region of East Africa. Males can grow to 23 cm in length.

South African bullfrogs are well known for their tendency to fight with each other. Tooth-like projections on their jaws are their primary weapon. These also help them hunt

Bullfrog (*Rana catesbeiana*)

larger prey, such as other frogs and small rodents.

South African bullfrogs dig burrows into the earth during the dry season and remain there until the monsoon season brings rain. They mate during the rainy season, the males calling females with their loud croaking. As with nearly all frogs and toads, eggs are laid in still, calm waters. Male bullfrogs aggressively defend the eggs against predators. South African bullfrog tadpoles hatch after three weeks. At first, they are bright green and smooth, later becoming olive green with spots and deeply folded skin.In many parts of the world, bullfrogs are a culinary delicacy.

Leopard frog

The leopard frog (*Rana pipiens*) is native to most of North America with the exception of the Pacific coast.

They are primarily terrestrial, occupying swamp areas, meadows, forests and mountains. As is the case with most frog and toads, in order to mate and lay eggs, a body of fresh water must be nearby.

Leopard frogs are yellow green with dark spots. The pattern and definition of the spots varies by region. These slender frogs grow to 10–15 cm in length. Ribs and spine are clearly visible.

Leopard frogs seek out moist depressions in the earth during warm weather and hide there most of the day. At night, they hunt spiders, insects and small crustaceans. They will also leave their hiding places during a heavy rain to hunt. Although many are highly territorial, claiming a certain hunting area and living there most of their lives, they may expand their range if it is raining. This colonization of nearby territory allows the population to expand. Most, however, will return

to their original territory once the rainy season is past.

Leopard frogs living in the north will mate in March, migrating to the nesting area in large groups. Males sit in shallow water and attempt to attract females with their croak, which is a low, purring sound.

If a male succeeds in attracting a female, he will mount her while she lays up to 20,000 eggs in the mud beneath shallow, still water. The eggs are fertilized immediately. Tadpoles hatch within a month.

Leopard frog metamorphosis is highly dependent on local environmental conditions. If the temperature and water level are favourable, tadpoles will develop into adults within six months, but poorer conditions can extend metamorphosis to as long as two years.

Leopard frogs from southern regions have no regular mating season. Females are ready to lay eggs whenever there is adequate rainfall.

Leopard frog (*Rana pipiens*)

21

Poison dart frogs

Poison dart frogs (*Dendrobatidae*) were once thought to be a subspecies of true frogs. We know now that they are a distinct family.

Some of the most colourful and interesting frogs in the world are poison dart frogs. There are approximately 120 species, all of them small, some a little more than 15 mm in length, with the largest no more than 6 cm. They live exclusively in the tropical rainforests of Central and South America, ranging from Nicaragua into Bolivia and south-east Brazil.

In contrast to other kinds of frogs, poison dart frogs are most active during the day. They are identifiable by their typically bold, bright colouration and smooth skin. Their vivid colours are more like those of butterflies and coral reef fish than amphibians. Although not primarily aquatic, the toes of poison dart frogs are double webbed for swimming.

Many species of poison dart frog are highly territorial. They will defend their territory from invaders with loud vocalizations. Males will compete for territory against other males as well as with females and younger frogs.

Reproduction in poison dart frogs is particularly interesting. In contrast to other frog varieties, the females lay only a few eggs, hiding them in a secure, moist location, where the male who has fertilized them keeps watch. After the tadpoles hatch, the male carries them on his back to the nearest water source, where they complete their development.

There are two main varieties of poison dart frog. One group is less colourful than the other. These frogs live on the shores of small creeks and, with one exception, are not poisonous. The second group, the most brightly coloured, are extremely poisonous. Their colouration is primarily defensive, a means of frightening off enemies. If this doesn't work, a powerful nerve poison can be excreted through glands in the skin to paralyze attackers.

The poison itself varies widely in strength. For many species of poison dart frog, any amount of handling releases it in quantities fatal to humans. Only a few micrograms need to be injected into the human bloodstream to cause death. Several Native American groups realized its worth by rubbing the frog poison on the tips of the darts blown from dart guns, which is what gave these frogs their name.

Dye dart frog *(Dendrobates tinctorius)*

Dye dart frog

The dye dart frog *(Dendrobates tinctorius)* is one of the largest poison dart frogs, with an average size of 4 cm for males and up to 7 cm for females. Less venomous than some of the other poison dart species, the skin secretions of the dye dart frog were used by Native Americans to dye parrot feathers.

The dye dart frog is at home in north-eastern South America in lowland forests. Its colouration varies based on its habitat; even among the same species one dye dart frog is more beautiful than the next, ranging from blue to blue-black with yellow stripes, or black with large yellow spots on its head and deep, dark blue forelimbs and hind legs.

Yellow-striped poison dart frog
(Dendrobates leucomelas)

Males can be recognized by three, wider, more rectilinear middle toes and a larger area of webbing between them.

Males attract fertile females with a loud call. The females follow the males to burrows where each female lays just 8–10 eggs. Once fertilized, the male will care for the eggs and defend them from enemies.

After the tadpoles hatch, the males carry the tadpoles to one or more nearby bodies of water, some of which may be rain that has collected in the hollows of trees, and continue to guard the tadpoles there. Larger tadpoles often cannibalize smaller ones. Other food sources include plant and animal detritus, insect larvae and algae. After ten weeks the tadpoles are about 3.5 mm long and ready to metamorphose into adults.

Yellow-banded poison dart frog

The yellow-banded poison dart frog (*Dendrobates leucomelas*) is one of the most vividly coloured of all the frogs in this group. They grow to about 4 cm in length and spend most of their time hidden on the ground. Males are usually smaller than females.

The back of this slender frog is black with three broad, bright yellow stripes enclosing irregular black markings. The skin of the frog shimmers with a metallic sheen.

Reproduction is usually preceded by a "call battle" between the males, each of which lets loose with a loud, trilling warble until a female frog approaches and chooses her mate. While she is laying her eggs, the male brings water to keep the nesting site suitably moist, after which he fertilizes the eggs at once. The male stays at the nest for a day or two before leaving for two or three weeks. When he returns again it will be right before the eggs hatch. Like most poison dart frogs, the male will then carry the tadpoles to water, where they feed primarily on algae. After

Strawberry poison dart frog

The strawberry poison dart frog (*Oophaga pumilio*, formerly *Dendrobates pumilio*) is found in South America at elevations up to 900 m.

Strawberry poison dart frog (Oophaga pumilio, formerly Dendrobates pumilio)

Strawberry poison dart frogs are small, rarely growing larger than 2 cm. The name comes from the bright red colour all over its body. Rarely, a strawberry poison dart frog will be lighter in colour, or green or blue. The throat area is darker in males than females. Otherwise, they are indistinguishable from one another.

another two months, they are fully metamorphosed into adults.

Immediately after metamorphosis, yellow-banded poison dart frogs are only about 15 mm in length. They start out black, with black spotted brown banding. After about a year the brighter colouration appears. Unfortunately, these beautiful colours make them a highly desirably terrarium pet.

Reproduction and the tadpole stage are particularly interesting in this species. After laying six to eight eggs on a dry leaf, the female departs and the male visits once a day, bringing water to keep the eggs moist. After the eggs hatch, the female returns to carry the tadpoles individually to small pools of water inside plants like the pitcher plant (*Bromelids*), where each tadpole will grow up alone. Every day, the female returns to each tadpole in its plant and feeds it one or two unfertilized eggs. Each tadpole will have consumed 20–30 eggs within the six to eight weeks of metamorphosis to adulthood.

Tree frogs

These small, cheerfully chirping tree frogs (*Hylidae*) can forecast the weather! Who knew?

Most tree frogs and related species don't actually live in trees, although they are expert climbers. Sticky pads on jointed fingers and toes allow them to scamper up and down the reeds and shrubs that grow around ponds and brooks. Their digits have developed to grasp with well-articulated joints and glands that exude a strong adhesive.

Distinguishing skeletal characteristics of tree frogs include an arched spine and a particularly flexible connection between the tailbone and lower back.

The 600 species of tree frog live all over the world with the exception of the Antarctic. The majority can be found in South America and Australia, with relatively few species native to Asia and Africa. Europe is home to the namesake European tree frog (*Hyla arborea*). A South American tree frog species is particularly interesting, with the female carrying her eggs in a pouch of skin joined to the rest of her body.

Tree frogs range from 15 to 140 mm in length. They are almost always green, brown or yellow. Most males have a large, inflatable vocal sac.

Tree frog species vary widely regarding habitat. Some will live most of their lives in trees, while others prefer low bushes near water. A few species are fully aquatic. Many can dig as well as they can climb, with the true tree frogs (*Hyla*) using calcified spurs on limbs to dig deep winter hibernation holes or quickly burrow into the ground to escape danger.

European tree frog

The tree frog native to central Europe (*Hyla arborea*) is among the best known of the many hundreds of species of true tree frogs.

Approximately 5 cm long, the European tree frog lives in swampland, moors, water meadows and gardens. It hibernates during the winter in frost-free burrows dug deep into the earth.

Red-eyed tree frog (*Agalychnis callidryas*), Central America

Red-eyed tree frog (*Agalychnis callidryas*), Central America

Tree frog (*Hyla arborea*)

Giant tree frog (*Litoria infrafrenata*), Papua New Guinea

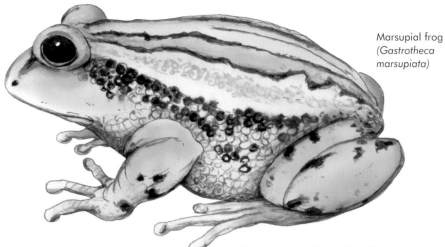

Marsupial frog (*Gastrotheca marsupiata*)

European tree frogs spend the months of March to June in water.

European tree frogs have a light green body with a white underbelly and a dark transitional stripe in between. Adaptations to different environments include protective colouration that may be brown, grey or yellow.

European tree frogs mate in April or May. The males start off with a loud chorus of croaking using their large, yellow-brown vocal sacs for amplification. After attracting a female, they climb on top and grasp her firmly for several days until she lays her eggs. Up to 1000 eggs can be laid at a time in gelatinous clumps. The tadpoles are ready to hatch after just 14 days. Metamorphosis is complete within a few weeks.

Tree frogs are primarily active at night, but will hunt a wide variety of insects during the day.

With its large eyes, glistening, brightly coloured body and finely articulated feet, the European tree frog makes a strong impression on the viewer. It is therefore one of the most popular amphibians in pet shops.

Marsupial frog

One particularly interesting tree frog is the pouched marsupial frog (*Gastrotheca marsupiata*) of South and Central America. Only 4 cm long, it is entirely arboreal, able to easily climb through the trees using the adhesive pads on its feet.

This frog stands out in particular for its unusual breeding behaviours. The female, always a little larger than the male, has a pouch of skin on her back in which to incubate her eggs.

The male mounts the female and fertilizes the eggs directly as they are laid. He then carries up to 200 fertilized eggs to the female's pouch and places them carefully inside. Once the eggs are all inside, the male closes the pouch.

After a few weeks, the female travels to a nearby body of water, where the tadpoles will develop. She uses one of her rear toes to open the pouch and push the tadpoles out into the water, where they will metamorphose into adults.

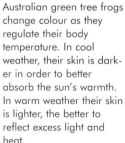

Australian green tree frogs change colour as they regulate their body temperature. In cool weather, their skin is darker in order to better absorb the sun's warmth. In warm weather their skin is lighter, the better to reflect excess light and heat.

Australian green tree frog (*Hyla caerulea*)

True toads

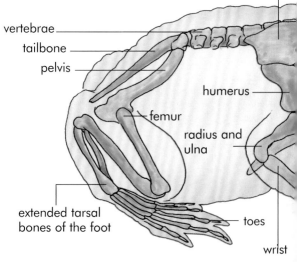

True toads (*Bufonidae*) live all over the world. There are nearly 300 species, most distinguished by plump bodies and thick, unarticulated legs. Toads grow between 2 and 25 cm long. Unlike frogs, all toads lack teeth and the pupils of their eyes are horizontal, instead of vertical.

Toads are famous for their wrinkled, wart-covered skin. Venom glands are frequently found in the folds of skin around the ears. These exude a mild, paralytic irritant along with slime that protects toads from enemies. The attacker has to attack the toad before it is affected: toads can't shoot the poison at an enemy like some frogs can. The most common toad poison is named after them: bufotenine. It is a mild nerve poison that attacks the brain and spinal cord, paralyzing the attacker. It also raises blood pressure.

Only very few toads are limber enough to quickly spring or jump away from enemies. Their heavy legs make their locomotion slow and laborious. Their digging ability, however, is enhanced by their anatomy. Their favourite place is a moist burrow just below the surface, although some species live in trees or water.

Toads eat snails, worms, caterpillars, spiders and insects, but no mice or other vertebrates. Their long tongues shoot out in the blink of an eye to capture their prey. True toads have been known to live for a very long time on very little food. Some toads live for 30 to 40 years.

Like most amphibians, toads mate, lay eggs and metamorphose into adults in water. There are also a few species that give birth to live young, a rarity among frogs and toads.

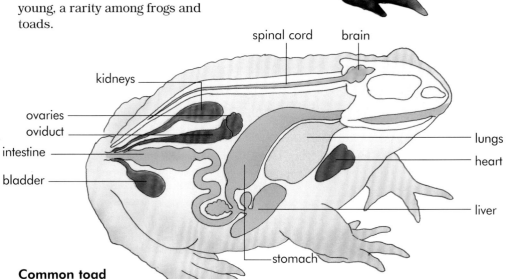

Common toad (anatomy)

spinal cord
brain
kidneys
ovaries
oviduct
intestine
bladder
lungs
heart
liver
stomach

Common toad

The common toad (*Bufo bufo*) is native to Europe, Asia and North Africa. Depending on habitat, it can grow between 12 and 20 cm long. The females are usually larger than the males. The common toad has a stocky body covered in warts.

Common toads spend the day hiding under rocks. As the sun sets they come out to hunt worms, insects, spiders and snails, waddling along and jumping every now and then to catch their prey.

Most common toads hibernate during the winter, re-emerging from

Golden toad (Bufo periglenes), rainforest in Costa Rica

Common toad (skeleton)

shoulder blade
vertebrae
tailbone
pelvis
humerus
femur
radius and ulna
extended tarsal bones of the foot
toes
wrist

their burrows in early March. Soon after, they migrate in large numbers to the same pond every year in order to mate.

American toad
(*Bufo americanus*)

Common toad
(*Bufo bufo*)

Females submerge themselves in water and exude gelatinous strands used to construct a nest in which they will lay thousands of eggs. The tadpoles hatch after ten days. They will stay in the pond for three or four months until they have metamorphosed into small toads that can survive on land. Toads can live for 40 years or more.

American toad

The American toad (*Bufo americanus*) lives in North American, south-eastern Canada and all over the eastern United States in forests, grasslands and gardens. They are nocturnal hunters, seeking out spiders, insects, snails and worms. By day, toads can be found hiding under gravel or in woodpiles. They also frequently dig burrows.

The American toad has a stocky body and is reddish brown in colour.

skull

eye socket

The skin is wart-covered. The American toad has a very broad head, also covered in warts. Females are slightly smaller than males.

During the mating season, toads gather in ponds and other still bodies of water. Between April and July the males attempt to attract females with a nonstop chorus of high-pitched, trilling vocalizations. Females ready to mate make a nest out of two strands of gelatinous

material, where they their eggs. They then leave the water. American toads lay up to 8,000 eggs that hatch after just one week of incubation. Like adult toads, toad tadpoles are protected from enemies by venom glands, which means fish rarely eat them. The tadpoles are fully metamorphosed into adult toads within two months.

European green toad

The European green toad (*Bufo viridis*) lives throughout Europe from southern Scandinavia to the Mediterranean islands, as well as in North Africa and Central Asia. They prefer sandy terrain, and are primarily terrestrial.

Green toads are small, just 6–8 cm in length. Their bodies are light coloured with sharply delineated green spots that are paler in females than in males. The underbelly is white. Males have a vocal sac that

gets ample use during the mating season. Although they spend most of their lives on land, green toads still have vestigial webbing on their feet and, if necessary, can live for an extended period of time in shallow water.

Like most toads, the green toad is nocturnal, only occasionally hunting during the day. Its diet consists mainly of insects.

Mating season begins in April and lasts until June. The males migrate toward favoured nesting areas, which could be any still body of water nearby, including large puddles, swamps or old quarry lakes. They attract females with a loud, high-pitched, trilling call. A female can lay 10,000–20,000

eggs, with tadpoles fully metamorphosed into adult toads within eight to twelve weeks. Green toads are able to reproduce by their third year.

Green toad
(*Bufo viridis*)

27

Spadefoot toads & primitive frogs

Spadefoot toads (*Pelobatidae*) are represented by 83 species that live in Europe, South Asia and North America. Most are terrestrial, hiding in holes during the day or in burrows they have dug out with their powerful legs.

Spadefoot toads are closer to frogs than toads in several ways. Unlike other toads, they have slender, frog-like bodies and longer limbs. The name "spadefoot" comes from a horny protrusion on their inner side of the rear feet that allows the toad to bury itself quickly in the sand.

Rain plays an important role in spadefoot toad reproduction. If the ground temperature is right, and provided males have succeeded in attracting females, they will mate in large puddles of rain. Efficiency and speed are also evident in the development of their young. Their tadpoles are fully metamorphosed, from hatchling to adult, within just two weeks.

The spadefoot family includes the genus *Pelobates* (western, common, Syrian, and Moroccan spadefoot toads), *Scaphiopus* (southern spadefoot toads) and *Megophrys* (Asian horned frogs).

Primitive frogs (*Discoglossidae*) are actually a family of toads. They live in Europe, North Africa and parts of Asia. They occupy a wide range of habitats, from grasslands to mountaintops, always in or near a body of water.

Colour and markings vary according to species. All have a plain, pale underbelly. Their most distinctive characteristic is a disc-shaped tongue that is attached to the floor of the mouth, and therefore not able to shoot out and catch insects. As a result, primitive frogs crush their insects with their jaws, using their broad tongue to hold onto the prey. Insects and other invertebrates make up most of their diet. If danger is near, most primitive frogs can quickly submerge themselves in water.

Common spadefoot toad, (*Pelobates fuscus*)

Males in this family have no vocal sacs, so that their mating call is a low, rapid purr rather than a croak or trill. They can be heard most frequently during the evening and into the night. After mating, the female deposits her eggs in the mud beneath a body of water, sometimes attaching them to a plant. The eggs are not laid in a mass as with most other frogs and toads. They are laid one at a time, or in small batches that, unlike most frog eggs, are not attached to one another with slime or gelatinous strands. Tadpoles of this species are 25–35 mm. They are also very dark in colour with a single gill hole on the lower side of the body.

Fossil finds from the Jura Mountains suggest that primitive frogs and toads already existed more or less in their present form some 150 million years ago, and in North America as long ago as the late Cretaceous period (ca. 65 million years ago). European primitive frogs include the midwife toad (*Alytes obstetricans*). Mediterranean groups include *Discoglossus* (painted frogs) and *Alytes muletensis* (Mallorcan midwife toad).

Common spadefoot

The common spadefoot toad (*Pelobates fuscus*) is native to central Europe and western Asia. It prefers sandy ground and gardens. It is sometimes called the garlic toad due to a particularly pungent skin gland secretion.

The common spadefoot hides during the day, digging a hole into the sand. It is a nocturnal hunter, with insects and worms its primary prey.

Its body is shaped like a sack. Its colouration is green-brown with irregular dark spots. The skin is smooth and lacks warts, giving it a frog-like appearance. Also in common with frogs are the projecting eyes and vertical pupils. Like all spadefoot toads, the common spadefoot has a calcified, spade-like digging protrusion along the inside of its rear feet, as well as webbing between the toes. The common spadefoot grows to approximately 8 cm long, with the females slightly larger than the males.

The mating season is from April to June, with eggs laid in the still waters of lakes, ponds and large puddles of rain.

During mating, the male grasps the female firmly, fertilizing the eggs as soon as they are released. The female exudes a single gelatinous strand that serves a nest onto which she deposits up to 1000 eggs. The tadpoles hatch and soon reach a length of 10–15 cm. After a few weeks, they are fully meta-morphosed adults.

Midwife toad
(*Alytes obstetricans*)

Asian firebelly toad

The Asian firebelly toad (*Bombina orientalis*) is a primitive frog with a disc tongue. It is native to Siberia, south China and Korea, where it lives in still bodies of water and rice paddies.

Adults are about 5 cm long. The upper body is brown or green with grey to blue-black spots. Its underbelly is bright red.

If threatened, the Asian firebelly toad exudes a foul tasting, milky venom that acts as an irritant to mucus membranes of the mouth, nose and eyes of an attacker. The toad will also flip to scare enemies off by showing its red belly, rolling onto its back and stretching out both legs.

Mating season is between April and August. The males have vocal sacs and can be heard calling to females day and night. Unlike other mating frogs and toads, the males do not congregate, preferring to keep their distance from each other. They will claim a spot and hold onto it until the water level falls too low or other claimants take over.

During mating, the male mounts and clasps the female. Eggs are laid in clumps in the water attached to plant stems or under rocks. There are only between five and twelve eggs per clump. Tadpole development is dependent on the environment. Asian firebelly toads are sexually mature in their third year.

Midwife toad

Midwife toads (*Alytes obstetricans*) are primitive frogs with disc tongues. They are very interesting animals. Their call is high-pitched and ringing, which is why they are sometimes called bell frogs.

Midwife toads live in the mountains of central and southern Europe, hiding in cracks in the rocks, under rocks or in burrows they have dug themselves with their powerful front legs.

Entirely nocturnal, midwife toads emerge from their hiding places at dusk to hunt insects and other small invertebrates.

Reproduction takes place in spring, when males attract females with their high-pitched, ringing song. After mating, the male wraps the eggs in their gelatinous nesting strands around his hind legs and carry them around for weeks. After three to seven weeks, he deposits the nest in shallow water, where the tadpoles will hatch. They will spend the winter there and metamorphose into adult midwife toads only the following spring.

Chinese firebellied toad
(*Bombina orientalis*)

Other frogs and toads

The variety of colour and form among frogs is greater than with any other amphibian due to their exceptional ability to adapt to their environment.

African reed frog (*Hyperolius*)

African reed frog

There are more than 50 species of African reed frogs (*Hyperolius*), which, true to their name, are mainly found in Africa. They live in fresh-water rivers, lakes and streams among the cattails and reeds that line the shore. Like tree frogs, they have well-articulated toes with knuckles that help them grasp and climb. The African reed frog is closely related to the true frog group.

Argentine horned frog
(Ceratophrys ornata)

Argentine horned frog

This frog (*Ceratophrys ornata*) lives in Argentina. It is smaller than all other species of horned frogs and is a particularly good digger. It can burrow until it is completely underground.

Madagascar tomato frog

This frog (*Dyscophus antongilii*) lives only on the island of Madagascar off the coast of Africa. It belongs to a group of narrow-mouthed frogs that have teeth in both the upper and lower jaws. The male tomato frog is much smaller than the female.

Madagascar tomato frog (*Dyscophus antongilii*)

Snakes

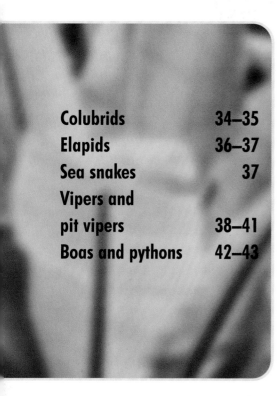

Snakes (*Serpentes*) are a suborder of reptiles. Among the over 2,500 species, most are found in warm and temperate zones. All serpents are descended from lizards. Over time, these ancient lizards evolved and lost their legs altogether. Instead of walking or running, they move forward by sliding or sidewinding. Only very few skeletons of early snakes show evidence of a pelvis or vestigial rear legs.

Most snakes can raise their heads up to 30 cm off the ground. A snake's skeleton consists of a skull, ribs and up to 435 vertebrae. A snake's extended body may be as small as 15 cm or as long as 10 m. Like all reptiles, a snake's skin consists of tough, horned scales.

Snakes have exceptionally good eyes, but lack retractable eyelids. This makes snakes look like they are staring hypnotically. Each eye has a scale eyelid for protection. A snake will slough off its outer scaly skin several times a year and can be seen rubbing against moss, heather, rocks and other rough places during a shed period.

Snakes also have a long, thin tongue that is constantly flicking in and out of its mouth. Although once thought to mean that the snake was ready to attack, we now know that this action is primarily associated with their sense of smell.

Like all reptiles, snakes lay eggs. In many snake species, development within the egg is so advanced that the young snakes leave the egg while still in the mother's body. Snakes that develop in this way are either born alive or hatch immediately after the eggs are laid.

Snakes are divided into different groups. These include grass snakes and water moccasins, pythons and boas, cobras, sea snakes and pit vipers.

Colubrids

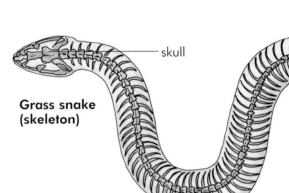

Characteristic spots on the back of the head

grass snake (Natrix natrix)

Over two-thirds of all snake species are *Colubridae*, nearly all of which are non-venomous. Colubrids can be found all over the world with the exception of very cold regions (as is the case with nearly all reptiles), parts of Australia and a few islands, such as New Zealand.

There are only a few characteristics that are common to all of the 2,500 species of this exceptionally large and diverse family of snakes. Unlike boas and pythons, colubrid skeletons show no sign of a pelvic girdle or any other trace of rear limbs. Colubrids also have long, whip-like tails and heads clearly distinguished from the rest of the body by a neck. Anatomically, each species has a vestigial or missing left lung and an over-sized right lung.

The lower jaw of a colubrid is relatively flexible, allowing the mouth to be opened very wide. Both the upper and lower jaws have teeth, but only very rarely have venom fangs.

Colubrids can live almost anywhere. Some live in trees, while others stay on the ground. Some dig burrows, while others are nearly entirely aquatic. Aquatic colubrids only live in fresh water. No aquatic

colubrids live in the sea.

Colubrid diets vary according to the habitats in which the snakes live. They are all carnivores, hunting insects and small mammals. Some species are highly specialized. The African egg-eating snake (*Dasypeltinae*) eats bird eggs, while the snail-eater snake specializes in eating snails in their shell. Colubrids kill their prey by constriction or by swallowing it whole.

Reproduction is also highly varied. The more exclusively terrestrial species in warm climates lay eggs. The aquatic species and those from cooler regions generally give birth to fully developed live young.

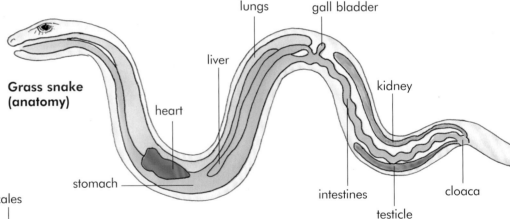

skull

Grass snake (skeleton)

lungs | gall bladder

liver

kidney

Grass snake (anatomy)

heart

stomach

intestines

testicle

cloaca

Cross section of reptile skin

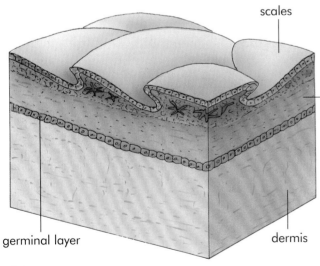

scales

epidermis

In contrast to amphibians, reptiles cannot breath through their skin. Instead, their skin consists of a tough epidermis and thick dermis that provide protection. The epidermis is covered with calcified scales or horny plates that vary from species to species.

germinal layer

dermis

Grass snakes

Humans have nothing to fear from the grass snake (*Natrix natrix*). Native to Europe, north-west Africa and western Asia, it is one of the most common and familiar of all snakes.

A grass snake is between 1 and 2 m long, with females somewhat longer and stronger than the males.

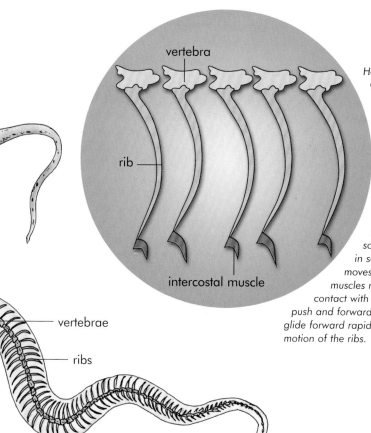

vertebra

rib

intercostal muscle

vertebrae

ribs

How do snakes move? Colubrid snakes have no shoulder bones, pelvis or limb attachments. They move sideways in a rippling motion or extend their bodies one rib muscle at a time and slide forward. A snake's skeleton consists of a great many vertebrae with pairs of ribs attached to strong muscles. When these muscles contract, the scaly belly rises off the ground in sequence, and the snake moves slightly forward. As the rib muscles relax, the snake is again in contact with the ground, giving it a slight push and forward momentum. A snake can glide forward rapidly by means of this rippling motion of the ribs.

Grass snake
(*Natrix natrix*)

Mangrove snake
(*Boiga dendrophila*),
South-east Asia, Indonesia
and the Philippines

Corn snakes

Markings vary widely between the nine different species of grass snake.

Most grass snakes hunt during the day on both land and water, seeking out fish, frogs, small mammals and insects. These are usually killed by constriction, but some species secrete a mildly poisonous slime that is deadly for its small prey, but harmless to humans.

The mating season for grass snakes begins in the early summer when the males attempt to attract females by rubbing their necks over their bodies. If the female responds, male and female entwine and mate.

After some two months, females lay about 30 well-developed eggs in a protected spot under moss or fallen leaves. After another one to two months, if the temperature is right, the young snakes hatch. They are about 15 cm long at birth.

Corn snakes (*Elaphe guttata*) are native to North America from the southern USA to central Mexico. They live in forests, but also in farmland, and always near a body of water. During the day they hide in woodpiles, under rocks, in abandoned houses or in any other suitably protected place.

Corn snakes can grow to over 1.8 m in length. Their colouration and markings vary within a range of red, orange, brown and grey. Markings are usually large, irregular spots in red, grey or brown, always outlined in black. Depending on habitat, the colours may be dull or vivid.

Corn snakes emerge from their dens at dusk to hunt birds, other reptiles, bats and small rodents. They strangle their prey via constriction before ingesting it whole.

Corn snakes mate in late spring, when females will lay up to 20 eggs. The young snakes, already more than 40 cm long, hatch during the late summer.

The name "corn snake" comes from their colouration, which resembles that of certain varieties of maize (Indian corn).

Corn snake
(*Elaphe guttata*)

Elapids

Snakes of the family *Elapidae* live in tropical and subtropical regions of Australia, Asia, North and South America and Africa (with the exception of Madagascar). The majority of species live in Australia.

The 250 or so species of elapids thrive in a wide variety of habitats. Most are terrestrial or live in trees. Elapids include cobras, mambas, coral snakes and kraits. Fifty species of elapid are aquatic, with some living in the ocean and others confined to freshwater lakes and rivers.

Size, colouration and diet vary from species to species depending

Mozambique spitting cobra (*Naja mossambica*), Africa

The spitting cobra is particularly fascinating because its spits its venom rather than injecting it into its prey with its fangs. With one powerful exhaled breath, the spitting cobra can propel venom, which it has allowed to drip from its fangs, a distance of up to 3 m. The poison sprays into the eyes of attackers, blinding them.

on habitat. All have one or more poison fangs in the upper jaw. Fangs are elongated, sharp teeth. An internal channel with two openings runs along the curving frontal part of the fang. This channel conveys venom

from a gland near the root of the fang. Elapids have muscular control over how much venom is released, although only a little venom is enough to kill most kinds of prey. The poison fang is only rarely used for defence.

The upper jaw of an elapid has other teeth in addition to the fangs. Since the fangs are rigid and cannot move, the snake needs the other teeth to hold prey in place so that it can effectively inject the venom. Like all reptiles, these snakes shed teeth and grow new ones, but elapids are never without at least one working fang. A new fang grows when the channel connected to the venom gland grows together with the root of a new tooth.

The venom itself is usually a mixture of proteins that disable the bodily functions of the victim. The formula of the venom often targets the most important prey of a given elapid species within a habitat.

In tropical and subtropical zones, thousands of men and women fall victim to poisonous snakes every year. In comparison, deadly snakebites are relatively rare in Europe.

The cobra group of elapids includes spectacled, Egyptian (*Naja haje*) and spitting (Naja nigricollis) cobras, the latter some 2 m long. The king cobra (*Ophiophagus hanna*) of Africa, at 4 m, is the largest of the elapids.

Spectacled cobra

The spectacled cobra (*Naja naja*) attains lengths between 1.4 and 2.2 m. This cobra's name comes from markings on the back of its neck that resemble a pair of eyeglasses. Spectacled cobras are olive green or brown to black. When threatened, the cobra can rapidly spread the ribs near its head, enlarging the neck area. Its greatest enemy is the mongoose.

Cobras live primarily off mice and rats, but will also hunt birds, lizards, frogs and tortoises. The cobra kills with a single poisonous bite before swallowing its prey whole.

A female cobra lays up to 20 eggs some 70–100 days after mating. The eggs are laid in hollows of trees or termite hills. The young cobras hatch after 50–70 days.

Cobras are the snake species most associated with snake charmers. The cobras are not responding to the flute of the snake charmer, however, though it may appear to, but to the movement of the flute. Cobras, like all snakes, are completely deaf. The movement of the snake charmer's flute seems to put the cobra in attack mode, ready to defend itself against enemies. Many snake charmers only work with cobras that have had their fangs extracted.

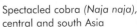

Spectacled cobra (*Naja naja*), central and south Asia

36

Green mamba
(*Dendroaspis viridis*)

Green mamba

The green mamba (*Dendroaspis viridis*) is native to what remains of the West African rainforest, living in the taller trees within the densest part of the forest. Green mambas almost never leave their home tree.

The olive-to-dark green colouration of the green mamba provides excellent camouflage in its habitat among the tree leaves. Mambas grow up to 2.5 m long and are fast and skilful climbers. Their diet includes birds and small mammals.

The green mamba is fairly shy. When threatened, its first response is to flee rather than attack. Its venom is a strong paralytic that asphyxiates its victim. Although the bite wound is small and not particularly painful, the green mamba's venom makes it one of the most deadly of all snakes.

Sea snakes

There are 50 species of sea snake inhabiting the coastal waters of the Pacific and Indian Oceans. Their habitats are exclusively aquatic and, with the exception of one species, sea snakes never go on land.

Sea snakes (*Hydrophiidae*) are easy to recognize by their paddle-shaped tails. The paddle tail propels them through the water, making them look more like eels than snakes. With the exception of the pelagic yellow-bellied variety, most sea snakes live in shallow coastal waters. Although they must surface for air, during longer dives, sea snakes can also absorb oxygen from the water through the skin lining of their mouths.

Like other venomous elapids, the sea snake has long, channelled poison fangs in its upper jaw. It uses this strong poison to kill fish, its main prey.

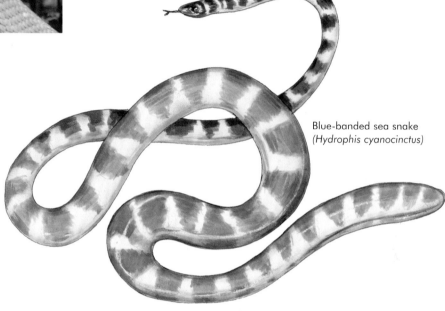

Blue-banded sea snake
(*Hydrophis cyanocinctus*)

Blue-banded sea snake

The blue-banded sea snake (*Hydrophis cyanocinctus*) has a wide distribution, from the coastal waters of the Persian Gulf to the Indian and Pacific Oceans and as far north as Japan.

Up to 2 m in length, it has a very small head compared to the rest of its body, with notably small eyes. Its nasal holes lie on the top of its head and can be closed by flaps of sponge-like tissue when the snake is underwater. Like all snakes, the blue-banded sea snake has lungs, but can remain underwater for up to two hours. Its rudder-like tail is well adapted to the aquatic habitat. Its rib musculature, however, is much less developed than that of terrestrial snakes, making it fairly helpless on land.

The vivid colouration of the blue-banded sea snake is particularly striking, with dark blue to blue-black stripes against a light background. Like all sea snakes, its primary diet is fish.

After mating, young sea snakes develop inside the body of the female. They are born live after two to six weeks. The blue-banded sea snake is one of the most venomous snakes in the world. Its bite kills many swimmers and divers.

Vipers and pit vipers

Vipers live all over the world with the exception of Australia, Antarctica and Madagascar. Most of the 40 or so species live on the ground, with only a few living in trees.

The true vipers (*Viperidae*) have a heavy body with a relatively short tail. The head is large and triangular. Scales, particularly on the upper body, tend to be smaller than in other kinds of snake. Most vipers have vertical pupils in their eyes.

The upper jaws of vipers carry one or more poisonous fangs, but no other teeth. Unlike cobras and elapids in general, viper fangs are hinged and flexible. When they bite, viper fangs snap forward. When not in use, the fangs are retracted inside a mucus membrane fold on the roof of the mouth. The fangs are hollow, with a channel connected to the venom glands. A bite from a viper stabs the victim like a dagger; the lower jaw plays no role at all. The fangs are not activated every time the snake opens its mouth; if that were the case they would get in the way of eating.

The fangs of a viper grow until new fangs replace them. Once the new ones are connected to the venom glands, the old fangs fall out.

Vipers come in a wide range of colours adapted for blending into their environment. Although their relatively stocky body makes them rather slow hunters, their bite is lightening fast. After they have bitten their prey, they release it and follow its scent until it dies from the poison.

Green pit viper
(*Trimeresurus albolabris*), India

The rhinoceros viper (*Bitis nasicornis*) is one of the most brilliantly coloured of all the vipers. It is nearly impossible to detect in its leafy habitat due to markings that make it almost disappear.

Rhinoceros viper (*Bitis nasicornus*),
West and central Africa

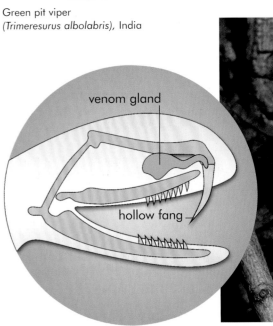

How does a snake inject its victim with venom? When the snake bites, the venom is injected through its fangs. In vipers, these are usually retracted into a mucus membrane on the roof of the mouth. When the snake is defending itself or attacking its prey, a complex lever system unhinges the fang until it is vertical and ready to bite. Venom travels through the fang through a channel connected to the venom glands in the snake's head. The venom is strong enough to paralyze or kill the prey.

This protects the snake from having to waste energy or risk injury by fighting with wounded prey.

Pit vipers (*Crotalidae*) are a separate family with even more highly developed mechanisms for venom delivery. They also have highly developed senses that allow them to track and kill their prey at night, even in total darkness. Pit vipers do this with a highly specialized sense organ located between the nostrils and the eyes. This thin membrane is full of nerve endings that allow the snake to sense subtle body heat waves emanating from a potential victim.

Reproductive behaviour is highly varied from viper to viper. Most viper eggs develop fully within the female's body, with young snakes hatching almost immediately after the eggs are laid. Only one or two viper species

Gabon viper *(Bitis gabonica)*, West and central Africa

The Gabon viper, also known as the puff adder, opens its mouth wide to display its deadly poison fangs.

lay eggs right after fertilization.

Viper venom is an enzyme that attacks the blood vessels and other organs in the circulatory systems, causing blood to flow into the body tissues so that the prey dies from internal bleeding. Another enzyme in the venom breaks down the tissues to pre-digest them even before the viper has begun consuming its prey. Some species of viper have venom that stops blood from clotting. This massive attack on the body tissues means that humans and animals bitten by vipers suffer severe symptoms at the bite site. If not treated, a painful death results as the blood vessels are destroyed and the circulatory system collapses.

European viper *(Vipera berus)*

European viper

The European viper (*Vipera berus*), also known as the European adder, is the most common poisonous snake in Europe. Its most distinctive features are the saddleback markings that run in a continuous band from the neck to the tail.

The European viper grows to about 1 m, with males somewhat smaller than females. They live primarily in moist but sunny habitats on the edge of forests, but also in meadows and fields. They have been found in mountains at elevations over 2,000 m and even higher in the more southern parts of its distribution.

The European viper eats lizards, frogs, mice, birds and insects. It is relatively slow moving and lives on the ground. It cannot climb.

The mating season for European vipers begins in late summer, initiated by a series of battles between males. This involves males "standing up" high, with their upper bodies swaying as they attempt to push rival males to the ground. Young European vipers are born live, just three to ten per year. The eggs fully develop and hatch inside the mother's body. Like most viper species, European vipers are born with fully operational fangs for injecting venom.

European vipers hibernate for the winter when the temperature falls below 8 °C. Most spend the winter in a burrow, a cave or under rocks. European vipers occupy a wide range of habitats from Siberia to the Atlantic and the southern Mediterranean. The only European country without a viper is Ireland.

Diamondback rattlesnake

The eastern variety of the diamondback rattlesnake (*Crotalus adamanteus*) is native to the south-eastern United States. They are most commonly found in forest clearings with sandy soil. Eastern diamondbacks are also excellent swimmers. The western diamondback rattlesnake (*Crotalus atrox*) is a close relative.

The eastern diamondback is the largest of all the rattlesnakes, reaching a length of 2 m or in rare cases even 2.5 m. They are massive, weighing about 10 kg. The head characteristically broadens at the base and is triangular in shape. Like all pit vipers, the diamondback has a special organ between the eyes and nostrils that allow it to locate prey by sensing its body heat.

The base colour of the eastern diamondback is dark brown, olive green or grey. The markings on its upper side are distinctive, darker coloured lozenges with a lighter outline. Two light-coloured stripes run

Western diamondback rattlesnake (*Crotalus atrox*), northern Mexico and south-western United States

along each side of the head, terminating at the eyes. The snout area is also lightly striped. The tail of a rattlesnake is marked by a black-white or black-grey sequence of rings. These are always hollow and make a rustling, rattling sound as the snake moves. If a rattlesnake is threatened, it stands up on its lower body, looks the enemy straight in the eye and backs up in retreat, rattling its tail loudly as it moves. Once the snake has made it back to its den, it disappears from sight in the blink of an eye.

A diamondback bite is extremely dangerous. Pit vipers inject a large amount of poison deep into the tissue of their prey, which is completely destroyed at the site of the bite. As blood begins to pool there, the circulatory system starts to collapse. Like many vipers, the rattlesnake bites its prey just once, then follows its trail until the victim dies.

Rattlesnakes hunt at night during the warm months of summer. Their prey is primarily rabbits, mice, rats,

interlocking segments

gophers and other small mammals, which it tracks by means of their body heat.

Rattlesnake young are born live, as many as 15 per mating season. They emerge from the female's body already 30–35 cm long and completely self-sufficient.

Eyelash palm pit vipers

The eyelash palm pit viper (*Bothriechis schlegelii*) lives in southern Mexico, Central America, and northern South America. It prefers rainforest and other moist habitats with thick vegetation. It is exclusively arboreal, climbing trees with the help of grip pads on it tail. This allows it to loop its tail around a branch while the rest of its body hangs free.

The eyelash palm pit viper grows to a length of 60–80 cm. It is recognizable by the horned scales ("eyelashes") above its eyes. Its colour varies from shades of yellow and green to brown. It may or may not have black or red markings forming a zigzag pattern from neck to tail.

The eyelash pit palm viper is entirely nocturnal. It lies in wait for its prey and then sinks its fangs deep into the victim, holding onto it tightly until it is dead. The entire time, it most often remains hanging on its branch. The favoured prey of an

All rattlesnakes are venomous. The ends of their tails are made of loosely attached horn rings. The rattling sound made by these rings as the snake reacts to an intruder warns the attacker, and should scare it off. The rattles of a rattlesnake's tail do not shed like scales. Instead, the rattles increase by one ring every time the snake sheds the rest of its skin.

Speckled pit viper
(*Trimeresurus wagleri*)

eyelash palm pit viper includes small mammals, birds and lizards.

Around 12 young eyelash palm pit vipers are born to a female per year, all born live and fully developed. Like their parents, the young snakes have grip pads on their tail. Many eyelash pit palm vipers live in Central America's banana plantations.

This leads to many accidental bites for the people

A key characteristic of pit vipers is the heat-sensing organ found between the nose and eyes.

Eyelash palm pit viper
(*Bothriechis schlegelii*)

who work there. Unlike diamondback rattlesnakes, these pit vipers never flee when confronted, but will wait until the last moment to bite. The bite is not necessarily deadly for humans, but contains a venom that can cause haemorrhaging or paralysis.

Speckled pit viper

The speckled pit viper (*Trimeresurus wagleri*) is native to South-east Asia, Indonesia and the Philippines. Its habitats are deep forests with thick vegetation near a source of water, and it prefers mangrove swamps and rainforests with lots of overhanging tree limbs. These vipers hang out over the water in the same position, nearly motionless, for hours on end. Like other tree vipers the speckled pit viper has well developed grip pads on its tail.

The speckled pit viper is easily recognized by its heart-shaped head, which is separated from the rest of the body by a neck. Adults are whitish or green-gold with dark perpendicular stripes. In some of its habitats, the markings are bright green instead of black. The belly of the snake is yellow. The heart-shaped head is also notable for the colourful markings around the upper and lower lips. Colouration is brighter and more vivid in younger snakes than in older ones. Every now and then, this otherwise arboreal species can be found slithering along the ground through high grass.

The speckled pit viper grows to a length of about 1 m. It is a plump, heavyset snake that only rarely bites. This unfortunately makes it a highly prized terrarium pet. They are also found living in snake temples throughout the region, worshipped by indigenous peoples who believe the speckled pit viper brings luck. Some will even move the vipers to nearby trees, from where they often make their way into houses.

The speckled pit viper lives off a diet of small mammals, lizards, frogs and birds. The young are born live, up to 25 at a time, during the spring.

Boas and pythons

Boas (*Boidae*) and pythons (*Pythonidae*) are native to all the tropical regions of the world and live in wet, forested habits.

Scientists who study reptile and amphibian taxonomy consider both boas and pythons to be primitive snakes because their skeletons still show lizard-like features that more recently evolved snakes do not. They have, for example, remnants of a pelvis and hind legs visible in their skeletons.

All boas and pythons are carnivorous. They attack their prey by biting them and then strangle the prey by constriction. Death usually occurs within a few seconds.

Boas and pythons are placed in separate families due to specific variations and characteristics defining each group.

A python is born: slowly and carefully the young snakes emerge from their eggs. It can take two days for a python to hatch. Python young are already 30–50 cm long at birth.

Carpet python (*Morelia spilota*)

Pythons live in Central America and the tropical regions of Africa, Australia and South Asia. They spend most of their time either in water or very near it. They can also climb trees and have grip pads on their tails. Among the best-known members of the python family are the king python (*Python regius*), the African rock python (*Python sebae*) and the carpet python (*Morelia spilota*).

All pythons are egg layers, with females depositing up to 100 eggs, which she wraps herself around securely, raising her body temperature to keep the eggs warm. It looks like she is expressing genuine maternal concern for her young. Pythons are the only reptiles that display this kind of behaviour. The female guards the eggs aggressively for three months, snapping her large mouth at anything that threatens to come near.

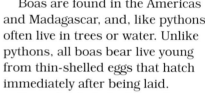

Green tree python (*Chondropython viridis*), north-east Australia and Papua New Guinea

Boas are found in the Americas and Madagascar, and, like pythons, often live in trees or water. Unlike pythons, all boas bear live young from thin-shelled eggs that hatch immediately after being laid.

Boas also lack the horny bone over the eyes that all pythons possess. They can also roll up their tails and have broad, shield-like scales on their bellies, most commonly arranged in a single row.

Carpet python

The carpet python (*Morelia spilota*) is a rainforest snake native to northern Australia and Papua New Guinea, although it is occasionally found in drier territories. It can usually be found in trees.

The carpet python is typically 2–3 m, but may reach up to 4 m in length. Its colouration varies widely. Its base colour can be yellow, beige or light brown according to its subspecies and population, with varying markings. There are banded, striped and spotted carpet vipers, with red-brown, dark brown or black markings. The range of colour and marking allow carpet pythons to lie in wait for their prey, well camouflaged within their environment. Their preferred prey is small mammals or birds.

During the mating season, the female lays eggs in a burrow or other protected location. The number of eggs is directly dependent on the female's age. Younger carpet pythons only lay around six eggs, while older ones can lay 30. Females coil themselves on top of their eggs and guard them. After 40 days the young snakes hatch, already 30 cm long.

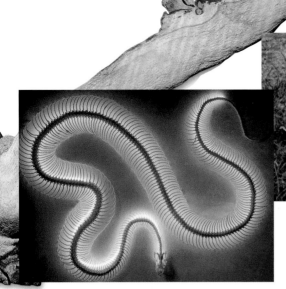

Skeleton of a python

Borneo python (*Python curtus*)

Boa constrictor

The boa constrictor, sometimes called the king snake, is the second largest snake in the Americas. It is native to Mexico, Central America and South America.

The boa constrictor commonly grows to more than 5 m long, and is one of the most beautiful of all the giant snakes. It is reddish-grey with large oval markings. These are usually light coloured and arranged in a zigzag line.

Boa constrictors can be found in deserts, but much prefer the moist heat of a swampy rainforest. They tend to stay on the ground but have also been seen in trees with their coiling tail wrapped around a branch. Like most snakes in the boa family, they are primarily nocturnal hunters, spending the day hidden out of sight.

Their diet consists of small mammals like rats and mice, but also includes amphibians such as salamanders and frogs. They also eat smaller snakes. They kill their prey by strangulation, first biting the victim with their powerful jaws and then wrapping around it tightly until it is dead. Boa constrictors bear live young

Boa constrictor

that hatch as soon as the thin-shelled eggs are laid. The young snakes are already 20–30 cm long at birth and completely developed. They begin to hunt shortly after birth.

Anaconda

The great anaconda (*Eunectes murinus*), a member of the boa family, is native to South America. It lives in river valleys and on sandy riverbanks.

With a length of up to 9 m and weighing as much as 130 kg, the anaconda is the largest of all snakes. It is not poisonous. All anacondas look more or less alike. The upper side is dark olive green with markings that consist of two parallel lines of dark brown spots. The underbelly is yellow with round black spots with a fleck of yellow in the middle.

Anacondas spend most of their day in shallow water waiting for their prey. If an anaconda sees a bird or mammal coming to drink, it attacks quickly and strangles it until it is dead. The giant snakes can stay under water for up to ten minutes before coming up to the surface to breathe.

Like all boas, anacondas bear their young live; the newly born snakes hatch from the eggs as soon as the female lays them in a protected place.

Borneo python

The Borneo python (*Python curtus*) is a rainforest snake native to the Malaysian peninsula and Sunda Islands. Its preferred habitats are swamps and riverbanks.

The Borneo python is 2 m long. Its colouration is yellowish to brown with glowing red spots, which are all different sizes. In its natural habitat the Borneo python is perfectly camouflaged. Its diet consists of small mammals and birds.

During the mating season, females lay 10–12 large eggs. The female snake then coil around the eggs to incubate them. By regularly contracting her muscles, the female raises her own body temperature by as much as 7 °C to keep the eggs at a uniform temperature and aid their development. If the eggs get too warm, the female will uncoil herself until the eggs cool. After barely three months the young pythons hatch, already 30 cm long. After hatching they are completely independent.

The Borneo python was once called the short-tailed python because its tail is strikingly short in comparison to its body length.

Anaconda

Lizards

With over 3,000 species, lizards (*Sauria*) are the most successful reptile group. They all have elongated bodies and thick, dry, keratinous scales. The dense, scaly skin keeps the lizard from drying out and protects it from enemies.

Lizards have four limbs, each, typically, with five toes. Some snake-like lizard species have underdeveloped legs that do not extend far from the body. The form and size of lizards varies widely. Unlike snakes, which are descended from them, lizards have rigid skulls and jaws with rows of pointed teeth on the edge of the jawline or just inside the mouth.

Most lizards are fast runners and skilled climbers. They may move forward in a fast crawl or slink along like a snake. Many can shed their tail if caught by an enemy. A new tail grows back within a few months. Like snakes, lizards regularly shed their skin, but in strips rather than all at once.

The lizard diet is based primarily on small animals like worms and snails. Larger lizards also eat small mammals, birds, amphibians, and fish. When the temperature is high, lizards can eat a great deal. This allows them to survive for a long time without eating if necessary.

Like all reptiles, a lizard's body temperature is dependent on the temperature of the environment. Body heat must be supplemented by outside heat, usually in the form of sunlight. In cold seasons, lizards hibernate. All lizards reproduce by laying eggs.

Among the 3,000 species of lizard are geckos, chameleons, and monitor lizards. Except for the Gila monsters of North and Central America, all lizards are non-venomous.

True lizards

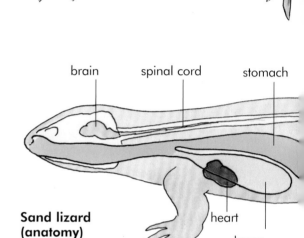

*Sand lizard
(Lacerta agilis)*

True lizards (*Lacertidae*) are slender, compact, fast moving reptiles with a characteristically long tail and well developed legs. There are roughly 150 species of true lizards in Europe, Asia, and Africa. Most live on the ground, although a few species prefer arboreal or cliff face habitats. Among the best-known true lizards are the mountain lizard, the green lizard and the wall lizard.

The familiar sand lizard exemplifies the anatomy of true lizards. It has an elongated body with a long tail that is round in section and ends in a point. Lizards are most active during the day, when they benefit from the sun's warmth and light. Sand lizards can be found near rail-road tracks, in meadows and in forest clearings, as well as hiding in the cracks of sun-warmed stone walls. Their skin is covered with scales that can be brown, grey or green, and may have spots or stripes as well. The colour of most lizards depends on the local habitat.

Lizards need very little water. Many species need little more than the morning dew that collects on leaves. They eat spiders, insects and larvae. In the winter, most lizards hibernate. They reproduce by laying eggs.

Lizards need a lot of sunlight. They often sun themselves during the hottest time of the day. The sun's heat gives them energy.

Sand lizard (anatomy) — brain, spinal cord, stomach, heart, lungs

Sand lizard

The sand lizard (*Lacerta agilis*) is native to Central and Eastern Europe, with a range that extends to Central Asia. It prefers warm, sunny habitats. Sand lizards are frequently found on hillsides, alongside railroad tracks or sunning themselves on dry stone walls. They can also be found low vegetation surrounding quarries.

Sand lizards are 18–20 cm long, with the males slightly longer than the females. Both males and females have a powerful body and thick head terminating in a blunt snout. Females and males have different colouration. Males have green upper bodies with a light-bordered dark brown stripe running from the head to the tail. The male's body on either side of the stripe is dappled dark and light with irregular spots, speckles, and dashes. Male colouration is most vivid at the beginning of the mating season, which can last well into the autumn months.

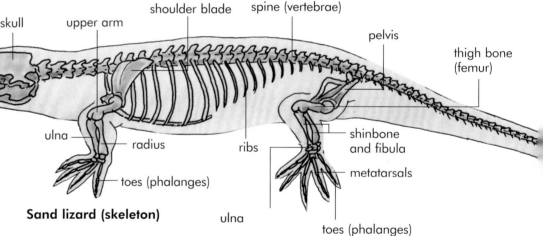

Sand lizard (skeleton) — skull, upper arm, shoulder blade, spine (vertebrae), pelvis, thigh bone (femur), ulna, radius, toes (phalanges), ribs, shinbone and fibula, metatarsals, ulna, toes (phalanges)

Female sand lizards are grey-brown with two light-coloured bands running from the head to the tail. The body on either side of the striping is covered with dark spots with a lighter-coloured interior.

Sand lizards live off a diet of insects, especially grasshoppers, flies, caterpillars, and similar species.

The mating season begins in late March, with the males battling each other for dominance. After mating, the female lays 5 to 14 eggs in a shallow depression dug into loose earth.

The young lizards hatch two months later. They are 6 cm long and completely independent from birth.

Adult sand lizards retreat into hibernation quarters as early as September, with the young lizards following in October. They spend the entire winter hibernating. Upon emerging in the spring, they shed their skin many times over.

Sand lizards are food for many other animals. Their enemies include martens, viper, and raptors, including hawks and eagles.

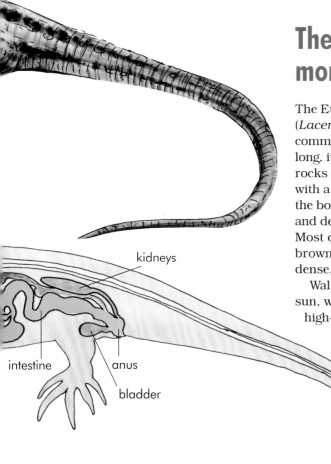

kidneys

intestine   anus

bladder

The European common wall lizard

The European common wall lizard (*Lacerta muralis*) is an extremely common sight. Growing about 25 cm long, it is frequently crawling along rocks and walls. Its body is slender, with a tail that is usually longer than the body. Colouration varies widely and depends on the environment. Most common is a red brown or brown base colour covered with dense, irregular black spots.

Wall lizards love the warmth of the sun, which they need to power their high-energy lifestyle. They scamper rapidly hunting insects, spiders, worms and snails.

The mating season begins as soon as the lizards wake from winter hibernation. The males engage in aggres-

sive battles for females. A male will try to frighten off competitors by raising his heads up high and exhaling to inflate his throat. After mating, females lay up to ten eggs in a hole in the ground and cover them with sand. The young wall lizards hatch after two or three months.

When threatened, wall lizards shed their tail. This distracts the attacker, giving the lizard time to flee.

Knob-tailed lizard (*Nephururus asper*)

Viviparous lizard

The viviparous lizard (*Lacerta vivipara*) is native to Europe and northern Asia. It ranges from Scandinavia and Great Britain in the north to Spain and Italy in the south. It is the only lizard known to live north of the Arctic Circle. It also occupies a wide range of habitats, including forests, wetlands, and meadows.

The viviparous lizard ranges from 14 to 18 cm in length. It is usually yellow-brown or grey. It has long, dark, lateral striping from its head to tail, surrounded by dark, irregular spots. Coloration and markings can vary widely depending on the environment.

Even compared to other lizards, the viviparous lizard is a highly skilled climber. It is flexible and fast, and can even climb underwater. Its diet consists of insects, slugs, worms, and other invertebrates.

Although it prefers wetland habitats, the viviparous lizard has been found living on rock faces at elevations of over 500 m. It can sit in the sun for hours without moving, calmly observing its environment. Generally a solitary creature, the viviparous lizard is only around

other lizards during hibernation and the mating season.

After mating, the five to ten fertilized eggs develop inside the body of the female, living off the yolk of the egg. After she lays the soft, thin-walled eggs, the lizards hatch immediately. They are fully developed and able to survive on their own. The viviparous lizard is also known as the mountain lizard, forest lizard or moor lizard.

Spotted thick-toed lizard
(*Pachydactylus maculatus*)

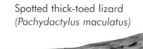

Geckos

Geckos (*Gekkonidae*) are lizards representcd by over 600 species distributed among the tropical, subtropical and temperate zones of the world. They live in deserts, forests and mountain habitats.

Depending on species, geckos can be anywhere from 5 to 45 cm long, although most are around 15 cm. Geckos have relatively flat heads and proportionately large eyes. Their skin is soft and typically covered by very small, well-articulated scales.

Geckos are also identifiable by their broad splaying toes. These have gripping pads and hooked claws that make it possible for a gecko to easily clamber up a very steep surface or even a perfectly vertical one. Running upside down across the ceiling is also not a problem.

One of the most common geckos is the Tokay gecko. Growing to 25–28 long, its preferred habitat is near houses, whose inhabitants often believe that the geckos bring good luck. The Tokay gecko lives on insects, other lizards, small birds

Knob-tailed lizard (*Nephururus asper*)

and mice. Geckos kill their prey with a bite from their powerful jaws.

Geckos are primarily nocturnal. During the night, at certain times of year, one can hear the males hissing their mating call. Female geckos are mute; they cannot make a sound.

After mating, the female lays three eggs, usually stuck to branches, under stones or hidden at the foot of a tree. Many geckos lay their eggs in the same place year after year.

Other gecko species live in the desert, including the desert banded gecko (12 cm), the flying gecko (15 cm) and the leopard gecko (30 cm). The majority of gecko species live in Africa and Asia.

Knob-tailed gecko

The knob-tailed gecko (*Nephrurus asper*), is native to Australia. It is one of the largest geckos in the world. Its preferred habitat is the rocky, dry desert of the northern part of the continent.

Knob-tailed geckos are yellow-brown in colour with light-coloured spots all over the body. This camouflages the gecko so well that it is nearly impossible to see it as it climbs over the rocks.

The namesake feature of this gecko is its stubby tail, which is very short and ends in a knob-like protuberance. The function of this unusual tail is unknown.

The knob-tailed gecko is entirely nocturnal, spending the day hidden in tunnels and holes in the ground. At night it hunts insects and other lizards.

Spotted thick-toed gecko

The spotted thick-toed gecko (*Pachydactylus maculatus*) is native to East Africa. It crawls along the ground, hiding under stones, leaves and among low vegetation. Its habitat is the same as that of its favoured prey: scorpions and smaller lizards. The spotted thick-toed gecko

Spotted thick-toed lizard (*Pachydactylus maculatus*)

is 12 cm long and is typically grey-brown in colour with sharply delineated dark spots. Its diet consists primarily of the crawling insects that share its habitat. It hunts at dawn and at dusk.

Like many lizards, the spotted thick-toed gecko can shed its tail when threatened. Although the tail grows back, the new tail will not be as large as the original.

Day gecko (Phelsuma)

The anatomical features used for crawling along the ground are somewhat undeveloped in this arboreal gecko. The day gecko easily climbs trees with the adhesive pads on its feet. Day geckos are 15–25 cm long.

Day gecko

Day geckos (*Phelsuma*) are native to Madagascar and other Indian Ocean islands. They live exclusively in trees, often close to human settlements.

As its name suggests, and unusually for geckos, the day gecko is active only during the day. They displaying a range of green tones, including olive green, grass green, turquoise and dark green. Most have vivid red spots on their backs and a few species add blue bands from head to tail. The green colouration camouflages these geckos among the leaves of the trees that make up their habitat. They can change all or part of their colouration to blend in with the background, adapting perfectly to changes in light and shadow.

Day geckos feed on insects and spiders. A rare omnivorous lizard, they also drink nectar from flowers and fruit hanging from trees.

Namib sand gecko

The Namib sand gecko (*Palmato-gecko rangei*), also known as the web-footed gecko, is native to the Namibian desert of south-western Africa. Its habitat ranges from sand dunes to coastal rocks and cliffs.

Namib desert gecko
(*Palmatogecko rangei*)

The Namib sand gecko is perfectly adapted to its harsh environment. If necessary, it can absorb the moisture it needs to survive through its skin from the moist onshore sea breeze or when a fog rolls in. It also licks drops of dew off rocks.

About 12 cm long, the Namib sand gecko is red-brown with irregular black spots on its back and a yellow underbelly. Its oversized eyes are ringed with yellow.

The Namib sand gecko is rarely seen. It lives on and under the ground. It has small adhesive pads on its feet and tiny claws with small flaps of skin between them, resembling the webbing of aquatic amphibians. The sand gecko uses this webbing to "swim" through the very hot sand, thus reducing bodily contact with the ground.

If temperatures rise too high or danger threatens, the Namib sand gecko quickly digs a hole and disappears, backwards, with its head just below the surface. If an enemy tries to extract the gecko from its hiding place, it swishes its tail back and forth and digs in deeper. The sand gecko also uses its burrow to hunt. If prey walks by, the gecko can emerge from the hole and seize it in a heartbeat. Their favoured diet includes termites, flies and other insects.

Chameleons

There are over 100 species of chameleons (*Chamaeleonidae*), all but one of which live on the island of Madagascar and the nearby coast of Africa. The one European species is the common chameleon, native to Spain and Portugal. All chameleons are lizards.

Most chameleons are arboreal, spending their lives in and among trees. The species are closely related and share many characteristics. The body is flattened on both sides with a head festooned with horns and combs. Chameleon eyes are large and protruding. Each one can rotate independently of the other, which is as striking as it is unexpected.

Chameleons have two or three toes per foot with adhesive pads and gripping claws that allow them to move easily from branch to branch. Chameleons also have a long, gripping tail, also with adhesive pads; they wrap their tails around branches for security or when lying in wait for prey. Unlike other climbing lizards, chameleons move deliberately and slowly.

They have a unique tongue nearly as long as its body. Chameleons can shoot it out and pull in prey in the blink of an eye. Insects are its favourite food. The sticky, club-like end of the chameleon's tongue ensures that prey cannot get away.

Chameleons can also change their body colour and markings at will. Although many lizards can change colour and markings, this capability is most developed in chameleons. This allows it to approach prey nearly undetected. It can also change colour in response to heat or cold, or to escape an attack. If its body temperature drops too quickly, or if attacked, a complex physical and chemical process begins. The Pigment cells in the skin react to pigment-stimulating cells throughout the nervous system. Stimulation of the nervous system causes the pigmented skin cells to expand or contract, thus changing the chameleon's skin colour and markings.

Female chameleons lay eggs a hole she has dug. Some chameleon species bear their young almost live, with fully developed young chameleons hatching immediately after the eggs are laid.

Carpet chameleon (*Chamaeleo lateralis*)

Carpet chameleon

Like most chameleons, the carpet chameleon (*Chamaeleo lateralis*) is native to Madagascar, where it is most common on the high plateau in the island's centre.

The carpet chameleon is 16–20 cm long. When at rest, it is green in colour, with dark bands running around the tail and a few dark rings on the sides of the body. When excited, the carpet chameleon changes its colour and markings. Very rapidly its skin takes on a net-like pattern in shades of light blue, yellow, white and black.

When it wakes up from a nap, the carpet chameleon crawls onto a branch and warms itself in the sun.

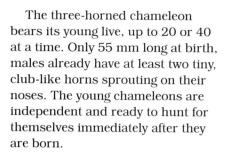

Three-horned chameleon
(*Chamaeleo jacksonii*)

Three-horned chameleon

The three-horned chameleon (Chamaeleo jacksonii), also known as Jackson's chameleon, is at home in the east African countries of Uganda, Kenya, Tanzania and Mozambique.

Males bear the characteristic three horns on the front of their face attached to the top of their nose. Females have at least one horn, and may have an attachment site for a second one. At 11–12 cm, the horned chameleon is small and pale green in colour. This allows it to be well concealed in its primary habitat, a thick moss that grows on tree trunks.

The three-horned chameleon bears its young live, up to 20 or 40 at a time. Only 55 mm long at birth, males already have at least two tiny, club-like horns sprouting on their noses. The young chameleons are independent and ready to hunt for themselves immediately after they are born.

Flap-necked chameleon

The flap-necked chameleon (*Chamaeleo dilepis*) lives in the tropical habitats of southern Africa, primarily in low trees and shrubs.

It is 25–35 cm long and gets its name from the flaps of skin hanging from the back of its head. If another member of its species approaches, the skin flaps stand up in a threatening manner. The flaps can also be raised one at a time.

The flap-necked chameleon is a master of adapting its skin colour and markings to the local environment. If it is sitting on a shrub leaf, it is green. When it is crawling along branches and twigs, its colour changes to red-brown. If attacked or otherwise excited, it turns dark green-black with light coloured spots. The flap-necked chameleon is one of the most aggressive of all chameleons.

The flap-necked chameleon will only leave its tree if absolutely necessary or to lay its eggs. Females dig a hole in the ground and lay 30–40 eggs, covering them with twigs. The young hatch after three months.

Its worst enemy is the boomslang, a highly venomous snake in the colubrid family. The chameleon's defensive behaviour of raising its head flaps to scare off an attacker has no effect whatsoever on the boomslang.

As its body temperature rises, the carpet chameleon disappears back into the shadows, where its camouflage is perfect.

Flap-necked chameleon
(*Chamaeleo dilepis*)

Iguanas

There are more than 600 species of the lizard family called iguana (*Iguanidae*) Most are found in North, Central and South America. They range in size from just 10 cm to more than 2 m in length. With one exception, the marine iguana of the Galapagos Islands, iguanas live on the ground and in trees. This gives them a wide range of habitats, from forests to mountains. Some even live inside houses. Iguanas have long, powerful bodies with extremely well developed limbs that are proportionately long compared to those of other lizards.

Most iguanas have physical features like throat flaps in addition to head and back combs or crests, the latter

usually extending all the way down the tail. These come into play when rivals threaten to take over territory or a predator attacks. When threatened, a male iguana shows the attacker its broad side. It then raises its neck and back combs while opening its mouth wide. When in attack mode, an iguana's typically dark colours become brighter, often with colourful spots. Iguanas live off insects, worms and snails.

At first glance, iguanas are easily confused with the family of dragon lizards known as *Agamidae*. They are, however, not closely related, and occupy completely different regions

Iguana

and habitats. As an example, although both dragon lizards and iguanas have teeth, dragon teeth grow from the outer side of the jawbone, and therefore they cannot regrow after a tooth is damaged or lost. Iguana teeth, in contrast, grow from the inner side of the jawbone, where new teeth can form to regularly replace old ones.

Green iguana

The green iguana (Iguana iguana) is native to Central and South America. As its name suggests, it is green. When young, the green is light coloured. As green iguanas age, the green becomes darker.

A green iguana can grow to be 2 m long. It has a long, spiny comb running from the head to the tail. Males and females both have a large throat sac that is always visible.

Green iguanas are primarily found in well-watered forests. They are good climbers and can also swim. Like many iguana species, their diet

Green iguana
(*Iguana iguana*)

is largely vegetarian. They eat plants easily harvested with their razor-sharp teeth.

In the autumn, females dig a hole and lay up to 40 eggs. The young iguanas hatch after three months. When small, they live mostly off insects.

If attacked, green iguanas defend themselves with their tails. A threatened iguana will inflate itself, hiss and wave its powerful tail around like a whip. If this is not enough to drive the attacker away, the iguana will bite.

In addition to attacks by its natural enemies, green iguanas also live in fear of humans, who consider its meat a delicacy. Iguana eggs and skins are also prized. Green iguanas can live for ten years or more.

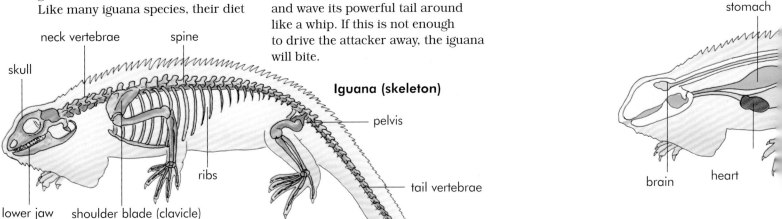

Iguana (skeleton)

skull · lower jaw · neck vertebrae · shoulder blade (clavicle) · spine · ribs · pelvis · tail vertebrae

stomach · brain · heart

Marine iguana (*Amblyrhynchus cristatus*)

Marine iguana

The marine iguana (*Amblyrhynchus cristatus*), native only to the Galapagos islands, is one of the most interesting animals in the world. It is the only lizard that goes into the sea to feed. It swims and dives to the bottom to harvest water plants and algae growing on the rocks. Glands in its nostrils help it expel the excess salt taken in from their maritime diet.

The marine iguana cannot breathe while it is underwater. To compensate for the lack of oxygen, it reduces its heart rate so that its blood pressure is drops and the oxygen in

its blood last for a longer period of time.

During the mating season, males battle over females. They often claim a rock opposite a rival and try to drive him away.

Females dig a shallow depression in the sand to lay eggs, covering them with sand. After four months, the young iguana hatch. Over the past several years, the numbers of marine iguanas have sharply declined.

Chuckwalla

The chuckwalla (*Sauromalus obesus*) lives in the south-western United States and Mexico. It prefers dry, rocky habitats. The chuckwalla loves the warmth of the sun. It is active during the day and hides itself in caves and between rocks at night. In the morning, it warms up in the sun once more and sets off to find

food. Leaves, buds and flowers are its favourites. The chuckwalla is sturdy and powerful, growing to 30–40 cm. The males are dark with a light yellow tail and a body covered in red or grey spots. Females and young animals are olive-grey or yellow-grey, frequently with dark stripes.

The chuckwalla is very well adapted to its dry environment. The folds of its skin hide lymph glands that keep the animal moist.

When danger threatens, the chuckwalla hides in cracks in the rock, inflating itself to make it impossible for anything to pull it out of its hiding space. Chuckwallas reproduce by laying eggs.

Chuckwalla (*Sauromalus obesus*)

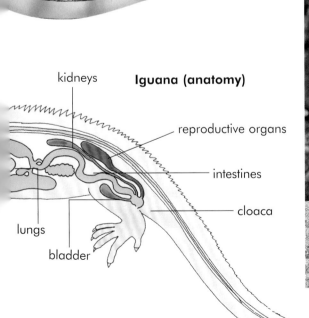

Iguana (anatomy)

kidneys

reproductive organs

intestines

cloaca

lungs

bladder

Monitor lizards

Monitor lizards (*Varanidae*) are the largest lizards alive on earth today. More than 30 species live in Africa, Australia, Indonesia and South Asia.

Although they vary widely in size from 20 cm to more than 3 m long, they all have the same elongated body type with a proportionately long neck and tail. Legs are particularly developed. Most monitors can both run fast and climb exceptionally well. They are also good swimmers.

Monitors have forked tongues that extend well beyond the animal's wide-open mouth. Both the tongue and ability to unhinge its jaws suggest a close evolutionary relationship with snakes.

All monitor lizards are meat eaters. The smaller varieties are satisfied with insects, smaller lizards and small mammals. The larger monitor lizards, however, eat almost anything, including frogs, crabs, birds and rodents. Komodo dragons can eat mammals the size of wild pigs. Monitor lizards also eat eggs laid by turtles, tortoises and crocodiles. Most monitor lizards will scavenge for carrion as well.

The mating season is marked by battles between rival males. When fighting, a monitor will stand on its hind legs and attempt to throw down the opponent. After mating, females lay between 7 and 57 eggs in a pit dug into the earth or in the hollow of a tree.

When enemies attack a monitor, it vigorously defends itself with its sharp teeth and pointed claws, and will strike out with its heavy, muscular tail. The only enemies monitors have to fear are humans who dine on its flesh and consider monitor eggs to be a delicacy. Monitor lizards are also hunted for their skins and fat, the latter a common ingredient in medicines.

Komodo dragons (Varanus komodoensis)

Komodo dragons

Komodo dragons are the largest lizards in the world. They are found on the Indonesian island of Komodo and a few neighbouring islands. Komodo dragons can grow to 3 m long with a powerful body and thick, long, muscular tail. The muscular limbs terminate in sharp claws. Despite its weight, which can reach 100 kg or more, it is a skilful climber and agile swimmer.

Komodo dragons have dark, scaly skin, although individual colouration varies, and can be more or less dull.

The large, sharp teeth and ability to both unhinge its jaws and open its throat wide means that Komodo dragons can hunt and devour animals as large as wild pigs or deer.

The number and variety of prey available to the dragons has greatly decreased due to competition with human populations that hunt the same animals.

scales, while others have huge flaps of skin around the head and neck. Bearded varieties exist, and many have a tail comb. All of these features come into play when the agama needs to defend itself from enemies or contend with rivals during the mating season. At rest the colours

Dragón de Komodo (Varanus komodoensis)

Komodo dragons are threatened with extinction and are currently protected by a wide range of conservation measures. Although they rarely directly attack humans, population pressures have led to a few deadly encounters.

Female Komodo dragons lay up to 15 eggs in a pit dug into the earth.

Agamas

Several of the 300 species of the lizard family of agamas (*Agamidae*) are also commonly known as dragon lizards due to features that cause them to resemble fairy tale dragons. Most are native to South Asia, where they live on the ground, surviving even in the driest desert and grasslands. The few species that live in wetlands may also climb trees.

Agamas are about 35–40 cm long. They have a notably long tail that is often twice the length of the rest of its body. They have well developed limbs that are proportionately long compared to those of other lizards. Several species are even able to run on two legs for short periods.

Colour and markings vary widely with species. Many have spiked

Agama

are dull, but when excited, its colours are bright and vivid. In some species the colour change only affects the head.

Agamas are egg layers. They use their long, whip-like tails in defence but, unlike other lizards, most agama species do not have the ability to shed and regenerate a tail if attacked.

Rainbow agama

The rainbow agama (*Agama agama*) lives in central Africa in tropical rainforests and the savannah, occasionally straying into settlements and houses. All they need to survive are ample hiding places and a high population of insects, their preferred food. Rainbow agamas are 10–14 cm long not including the tail. Females are a little smaller than males.

Unlike most reptiles, rainbow agamas are social animals, living in groups of up to 25 lizards occupying a well-defended territory. The strongest male is in charge. He is usually in the company of the strongest female, who may drive other females away. The rest of the colony consists of young rainbow agamas or low ranked adult females. If another male challenges the leading male, he responds with a threatening posture and loud hissing.

Rainbow agama
(*Agama agama*)

Rainbow agama (*Agama agama*)

head and parts of the tail turning bright orange. Females are generally brown with a blue-green pattern of spots from the head to the base of the neck.

After mating, females dig a hole in moist earth and lay between four and six eggs before closing the nest with sand. The eggs absorb moisture from the earth. Young dragon lizards hatch two to three months later.

Broad-headed skink (*Eumeces laticeps*)

If it comes to a fight, he will change colour. His body will become lighter and spotted, and his head will turn brown with a light stripe. The lizards will fight it out by swatting each other with their tails until one gives in. When the struggle is over, both males return to their duller, resting colouration.

When male rainbow lizards sun themselves in the early morning light their skin turns light blue, with the

Frilled lizard

The frilled lizard, also known as the frill-necked lizard (*Chlamydosaurus kingii*), is native to northern Australia and Papua New Guinea. It prefers forested habitats and spends most of its time in trees.

The frilled lizard is about 26 cm excluding its very long tail. An adult with its tail can be up to 90 cm long. Their diet consists of spiders, insects and small mammals. Frilled lizards are most active during the day.

Frilled lizards have yellow-brown to black scales. They also have skin folds attached to the front and sides of the head and neck. These can fully extend, looking like an enormous bowtie, during the territorial battles of the mating season or when predators threaten. When excited, its colours change from dull to brilliant, with vivid spots in red, yellow, black and white. In an adult male, the extended skin folds can be up to 30 cm in diameter. To increase the fear factor, a frilled lizard will extend its skin folds while standing up on its rear legs, flicking its long, whip-like tail back and forth. If necessary, frilled lizards can stand on their two rear legs and swiftly run away.

Frilled lizard
(*Chlamydosaurus kingii*)

Skinks

Skinks (*Scincidae*) are a large group of lizards represented by 800 different species found all over the world with the exception of the Antarctic. They prefer tropical and temperate environments.

Skink bodies are elongated, rounded and covered in scales so smooth that one of the other names for skinks is "smooth lizards." The scales are rounded in section, hexagonal in plan and attached to a thin layer of bone. A skink's head has several large, shield-like scales on the top, arranged symmetrically. The snout is usually pointed.

Some skinks are more similar to true lizards with well-developed legs and powerful feet. Others are more snake-like with vestigial or severely underdeveloped limbs. The scales of a snake and skink are very different. A skink's tongue is also very different from that the superficially similar glass lizards. Skink tongues are not anchored like glass lizard tongues, are not quite as long, and are curved rather than clubbed at the end. Skink tails vary widely from species to species.

Most skinks live entirely on land. Some dig burrows, while others live between rocks or in trees. Different species are highly adapted to their specific environments. Some have transparent eyelids, climbing spurs, adhesive pads on their feet and grip pads on their tails.

Most skinks eat insects and small animals. The larger skinks are all vegetarian. Two-thirds of all skink species reproduce by laying eggs, between 3 and 23 at a time. The rest bear their young live. Several skink species provide their young with a higher degree of parental care than most reptiles.

Skinks are divided into three subfamilies: 1) giant skinks (*Tiliquinae*), 2) true skinks (*Scincinae*) and snake-like skinks (*Lygosominae*).

Broad-headed skink

The broad-headed skink (*Eumeces laticeps*) is native to North America. It is a tree-dweller living in temperate forests.

The broad-headed skink has a powerful body and thick limbs with long, slender toes. The tail is long in proportion to the rest of the body and tapers toward the end. Like most arboreal lizards, the broad-headed skink is a skilled climber.

The skink's body is brown or greenish, with lateral banding on either side of a widely varying, lighter coloured pattern of irregular markings. During the mating season the head of the male turns bright red.

When a male broad-headed skink spots a rival, a battle for dominance begins. Skinks will attack each other at full speed with jaws open, ready to bite.

Blue tongue skink

The blue-tongued skink (*Tiliqua*) is found all over Australia. There are ten species and several sub-species. Its name comes from the cobalt-blue tongue, prominently displayed within its bright red mouth.

Depending on species, blue-tongued skinks can be between 15 and 52 cm long. They are powerful and stocky with a large head and

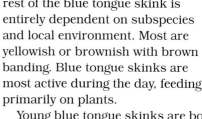

Blue tongue skink
(*Tiliqua*)

short, heavy legs. The colour of the rest of the blue tongue skink is entirely dependent on subspecies and local environment. Most are yellowish or brownish with brown banding. Blue tongue skinks are most active during the day, feeding primarily on plants.

Young blue tongue skinks are born live, roughly five to ten per litter. Young blue tongues are usually yellow with dark banding.

When danger threatens, the blue tongue skink inflates itself, sticks out its blue tongue and hisses. It is, however, all a show. Despite its mouthful of strong teeth, the blue tongue skink almost never bites. If the attacker is not frightened off, the skink will choose to flee instead of fight.

Other members of the blue tongue skink family (*Tiliqua*) include the bobtail (*Tiliqua rugosa*), Gerrard's blue tongue (*Tiliqua Gerradi*), the common blue tongue (*Tiliqua scincoides*), the mourning skink (*Tiliqua luctuosa*) and the glossy swamp skink (*Tiliqua luctuosa*).

Mating behaviour is complex, with set patterns and rituals.

After the female has laid her eggs, she engages in what is for reptiles an extraordinary level of parental care. The female watches over the eggs, regulates their temperature with her body and cleans them with her tongue. If danger approaches, she will defend the nest. She helps the young skinks hatch and tends them for several days afterward.

Young five-lined skinks have different colouration than older ones. They are dark black with a red or bright blue tail.

The five-lined skink

The five-lined skink (*Eumeces fasciatus*) is native to eastern North America. It lives on the ground in grasslands or underneath low brush.

The five-lined skink has a powerful body with strong limbs and long, slender toes. Its tail tapers toward the end and is twice as long as the body. The base colour of the body is brown or brownish green, with five lateral bands interspersed by light-coloured spots running the length of the body.

During the mating season, male five-lined skinks engage in violent battles for dominance, during which their heads turn bright orange.

Glass lizards

Blindworm (*Anguis fragilis*)

Glass lizards (*Anguidae*) are found throughout Africa, Europe and Asia. A few species, including the alligator lizard and the Costa Rican diploglossus ("two tongued") lizard, are found in Central America.

Glass lizards are slender and very snake-like, with a long tail that can be shed if there is danger. The entire body is covered with glossy, smooth scales attached to bone for maximum strength. Despite its otherwise dense scale pattern, glass lizards have glands in folds in their skin that play a role in breathing, laying eggs and hunting prey.

A glass lizard grows between 20 and 120 cm. It has movable eyelids and a blunt snout. All glass lizards have double-pointed tongues. Limbs can be so underdeveloped as to be barely present and entirely non-functional, as is the case with the glass lizard called the blindworm. In other species, the limbs are normal.

Glass lizards hunt insects, other lizards, small invertebrates and small mammals. Most reproduce by laying eggs, while others develop inside the mother's body, hatching the moment the eggs are laid.

The best-known glass lizard is the blindworm, a name often applied to the entire group.

Sheltopusik

The sheltopusik (*Ophisaurus apodus*), also known as the European legless lizard, lives in Europe from Greece to the Black Sea, and in south-west and central Asia. It prefers dry habitats and mountain landscapes.

The sheltopusik can grow to 1.7 m, making it the largest of all glass lizards. It has a powerful body, with anatomical remnants of limbs still present in the skeleton. It is usually dark in colour, with glossy, smooth scales that are rhomboid in plan, each anchored to bone. Folds in the skin are marked by less rigid scales. A sheltopusik's tail is longer than its body, tapering to a fine point.

Sheltopusiks eat small animals like mice and other lizards. Its strong jaws allow it to eat snails as well, shell and all. If larger animals approach, it rapidly spins around, hissing, in an attempt to confuse the enemy before throwing itself at it. It can bite, and can also spray foul-smelling liquid from its anus in defence.

Males are particularly aggressive during the mating season, when they will fight other sheltopusiks for access to females. After mating, the female lays five to seven eggs in a small, well-concealed burrow underneath a rock or tree stump. The female coils herself around the eggs and watches over them. After about a month, they hatch. Newborn sheltopusiks are 12 cm long.

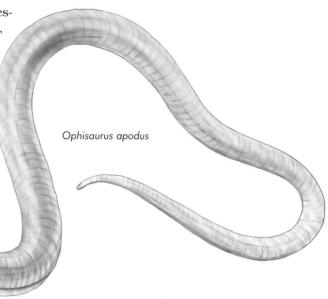

Ophisaurus apodus

Blindworms

Blindworms, also known as slow worms, are the lizards that most resemble snakes. These legless reptiles are still considered lizards because their skeleton retains both shoulder and pelvic bones.

Blindworms are native to Europe and are also found in parts of Asia and Africa. Their habitats are forests, grasslands and meadows.

Their colouration is red-brown to grey. Females have a black stripe on the back. Males have dark-coloured spots instead.

During the heat of the day blindworms hide under stones, emerging only in the early morning and evening to slither forward and hunt for worms, spiders and insects. Slugs are their favourite prey, making blindworms a useful garden predator.

Blindworms ward off aggressors by shedding their long tail. The tail always breaks off at the same spot, an anatomically predetermined "detach here" line. The tail grows back completely after a few weeks, but will be a little shorter with each regeneration.

Mating takes place in the late spring, but females will not lay their 12 to 20 eggs for another three months. The young blindworms hatch immediately. They are already 5–8 cm long and developed fully within the mother's body.

CHAPTER 5

Crocodilians

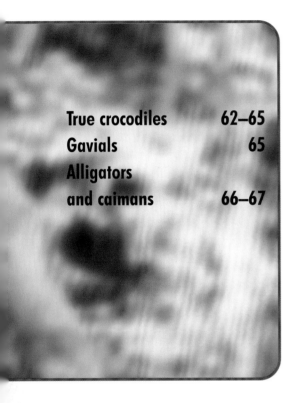

Crocodilians (*Crocodylia*) have the body type of a lizard, but are covered with horny scales or large, armoured plates. They evolved some 230 million years ago, but are today represented by just 21 different species, including true crocodiles, alligators and gavials. All are native to tropical and subtropical zones of the Americas, Asia, Australia and Africa. There are no crocodiles in Europe.

Crocodilians have enormous heads terminating in a snout that can be narrow and pointed or very broad and squared. The skull has two openings behind each eye to reduce the overall weight of the skull and provide anchorage for the crocodile's massive jaw muscles. With jaw muscles attached so far back, a crocodile can open its mouth very wide. This increases the already considerable strength of its bite. Crocodilians can also eat and breathe at the same time because the roof of the mouth separates the gullet from the nasal passages. The nostrils are also located much further back along snout, allowing crocodiles to breath through their nose even when the rest of the body is underwater.

Crocodilians are apex predators with few, if any, natural enemies. They spend most of their time in water, swimming forward with snake like movements propelled by their muscular, rudder-like tail.

All crocodilian species are egg layers (*ovipar*), with eggs that resemble goose eggs in shape and size. Females lay 20–100 eggs in a pit covered with sand or twigs. The mother remains in the area to watch over them. The eggs are incubated not by the mother, but by the warmth of the sun or heat generated from the natural composting of vegetation.

Cuban crocodile (*Crocodylus rhombifer*), Cuba

"Hissing" crocodile with wide open mouth

True crocodiles

Of the diverse ancient order of Crocodilians, only a few species survive today. Though they may resemble lizards, true crocodiles have a number of distinctive characteristics.

True crocodiles (*Crocodylidae*) can be distinguished from alligators and similar reptiles by the arrange-

Nile crocodile eye

ment of their teeth. The oversized fourth tooth of the lower jaw fits into a groove in the upper jaw, making it visible even when the mouth is closed. The other upper and lower teeth also fit precisely into gaps in the opposite jaw. In addition to the oversized fourth lower jaw tooth, the fifth tooth of the upper jaw is larger than the others in the row.

Unlike most gavials and alligators, true crocodiles have long, nearly triangular snouts. Along with the unique arrangement of crocodile teeth, snout shape is a good way to tell true crocodiles from similar reptiles.

Nile crocodile

True crocodiles are native to Africa, including Madagascar, Australia, the Sunda Islands, India, Mexico, and Central and South America.

The Nile crocodile (*Crocodylus niloticus*) is native to the large rivers, swamplands and lakes of Africa. Other crocodiles flourish there as well, including the slightly smaller slender-snouted crocodile (*Crocodylus cataphractus*), which has distinctive rows of armoured plating on its back and ossified plates on its belly.

Central and South America are represented by the relatively small Morelet's crocodile (*Crocodylus moreletii*), also known as the Mexican crocodile. It has a broad, curved snout with distinctive bumps and bulges in front of the eyes.

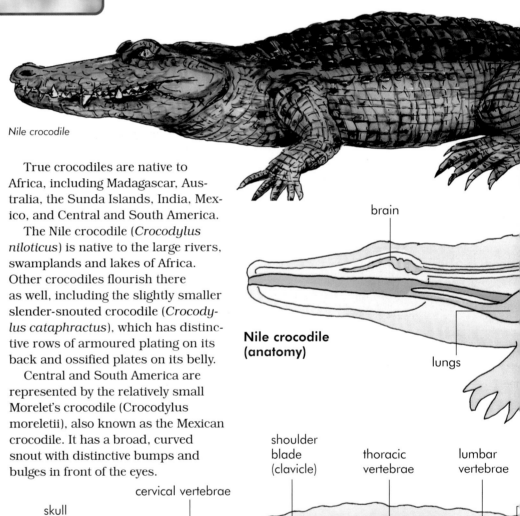

Nile crocodile (anatomy)

brain

lungs

Nile crocodile (skeleton)

skull

cervical vertebrae

shoulder blade (clavicle)

thoracic vertebrae

lumbar vertebrae

lower jaw

humerus

radius and ulna

toe bones (phalanges)

Huesos del tarso

A crocodile suns itself on the banks of a river.

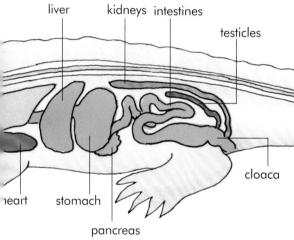

liver kidneys intestines

testicles

cloaca

heart stomach

pancreas

tarsal bones

caudal vertebrae

thigh bone (femur)

Nile crocodile

The population of Nile crocodiles (*Crocodylus niloticus*) has sharply decreased in recent years. Its skin is high prized by poachers. This true crocodile is native to Africa.

Lizard-like in its basic anatomy the Nile crocodile can be more than 6 m long. It has a flattened skull and powerful, rudder-like tail. Thick horn plates cover its body, but are densest on its back and attached directly to bone.

The Nile crocodile spends its nights in the water of lakes, swamp-land and rivers. During the day it climbs on land to sun itself. It hunts birds and large mammals by lying low just under the surface of shallow water with only its rear-set nostrils and tops of its eyes emerging. It can breathe and visually scan its environ-ment for prey with most of its body concealed underwater. When other animals come to drink, the crocodile snaps its powerful jaws and seizes its prey, holding tight with its numerous, long teeth as it drags the victim underwater, until it drowns. Once the prey is dead, the crocodile devours it, tearing off large chunks of flesh or swallowing it whole.

Nile crocodiles reproduce follow-ing a mating ritual that ends with the female laying up to 50 eggs in the sand. The eggs are large, approx-imately the size and shape of goose eggs. The female remains in the area of the nest for the three months or so until the young develop. When they are ready to hatch, they call to their mother from inside the egg with a soft quacking sound. The mother then opens up the nest and carries the hatchlings to water. The young crocodiles will hunt insects, fish and birds until they are large enough to hunt larger prey.

Nile crocodile (*Crocodylus niloticus*)

Dwarf crocodile (Osteolaemus tetraspis)

tle lighter with dark spots. The belly is dark and shiny.

The dwarf crocodile has brown eyes and an unusually shaped snout. Shorter than is typical for crocodiles, it is broad and flat, barely coming to a point at its tip. The forehead does not slope, but rises abruptly, with the horned plates over the eyes covered with bony ossifications. The neck is defined by a series of four humps perpendicular to the rest of the body. The overall impression is more that of a dwarf caiman rather than a true crocodile. Young dwarf crocodiles are

recognizable by their more vivid colouration. They are black with reddish-yellow stripes on the back and yellow spots on the belly.

Dwarf crocodiles live primarily on the hard-shelled molluscs that share their freshwater habitat. Little else is known about this rare crocodile that, in recent years, has been hunted to near extinction due to its valuable skin.

Dwarf crocodile

The dwarf crocodile (*Osteolaemus tetraspis*) is native to fresh-water habitats in West and central Africa. They prefer small river systems, lakes and ponds. At only 1.5 m, they are one of the smallest true crocodiles. They are dull black-brown in colour, with the head, back plates and tail crest a lit-

Saltwater crocodile (Crocodylus porosus)

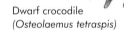

Dwarf crocodile
(Osteolaemus tetraspis)

Saltwater crocodile

The saltwater crocodile is widespread in South Asia and Australia. It lives in brackish water near the seacoast, but can also venture inland into rivers. It has even been sighted swimming on the high seas of the Indian and Pacific oceans.

Saltwater crocodiles grow to between 4 and 7 m long. They are dark green to green-brown in colour with yellow bellies. Two bony ridges running from each eye to the tip of the snout make them easy to identify. They usually lack horn plates in the neck region, where they have thick, but more flexible, scales instead. The horn plates along its back are organized into four rows.

Saltwater crocodiles can hunt very large mammals, including humans, who have long hunted the crocodiles for their skin. They remain threatened with extinction despite laws in place to protect and conserve the species.

False gavial (*Tomistoma schlegelii*)

False gavial

The false gavial (*Tomistoma schlege-lii*) gets its name from its misleading resemblance to the Ganges gavial, to which it is not related. The false gavial is actually a true crocodile (*Crocodylidae*).

False gavials live in the rivers, lakes and other wetlands of the Malaysian peninsula and the islands of Sumatra and Borneo.

Like the Ganges gavial, the false gavial has a long, narrow snout. Its teeth are those of a true crocodile, with the each jaw carrying just 20 or 21 total. A false gavial has a plump body and nearly rectangular head. It is dark brown with perpendicular dark grey stripes that widen to dark bands at the tail. The belly is light bluish grey to grey in colour.

The false gavial spends most of each day dozing in the sun or submerged in a watering hole. At night, it hunts for fish.

Local inhabitants revere the false gavial as a sacred animal throughout South-east Asia.

Gavials

Ganges gavial

The Ganges gavial (*Gavialis ganeti-cus*) is the only surviving gavial species. It lives in the great Indian rivers of Brahmaputra, Indus and Ganges.

In contrast to true crocodiles, the gavial has a very long, very narrow snout and hundreds of very pointy but relatively small teeth. As a result, the gavial is not able to hunt or consume very large prey.

As a result, although the Ganges gavial is large, and commonly grows up to 7 m long, it poses no danger to humans. It lives off frogs and fish, which it catches by rapidly slashing its head back and forth as it swims.

Ganges gavial (*Gavialis ganeticus*)

Gavials leave the water only to lay eggs. Females dig a pit to use as a nest on the banks of a river, and the eggs are laid at night.

Although the Ganges gavial is a sacred animal in India, it has nonetheless been hunted to near extinction for its skin. They are rarely seen today.

Alligators and caimans

Black caiman (*Melanosuchus niger*)

The alligator family (*Alligatoridae*) includes just seven species, all of which are native to tropical and subtropical regions of the Americas and South-east Asia. Only two species are true alligators; the other five are more correctly called caimans.

Alligators differ from crocodiles in several key features, most obviously in the arrangement of their teeth. Unlike the crocodile's, the alligator's enlarged fourth tooth in

the lower jaw is not visible when the mouth is closed. Instead of fitting into the exterior of the upper jaw, like a crocodile, the alligator's fourth tooth is inserted into a slot on the interior of the jaw. Alligators also generally have broader, flatter mouths and a snout area that tends not to come to a point like a crocodile's. Caimans, specifically, also have characteristic belly plates that are not fixed to bone, like those of crocodiles. Instead, they overlap like roof tiles and as a result are more flexible.

Alligators live primarily off fish, snakes, birds and turtles, with the prey either devoured whole or swallowed after being torn into to pieces by powerful jaws. Alligators cannot chew their food.

During the mating season male alligators have a loud call to attract females to their territory, which they defend fiercely from other males. They may engage in physical battles, but more often pretend to attack only to back off with their enormous mouths open in warning.

After mating, the male leaves the female. She builds a nest out of vegetative debris and mud. The average female alligator lays between 30 and 60 eggs. Females stay in the area to guard the nest, but rely on the heat of the sun to incubate them. After 60 days, the young alligators hatch. They stay near the mother for some time for their own protection.

The two species of alligator still in existence are the Chinese alligator (*Alligator sinensis*), a native of the Yangtze River, and the much larger American alligator (*Alligator mississippiensis*), found throughout the south-eastern United States.

Caimans are primarily tropical and most common in the Americas. The largest is the black caiman (*Melanosuchus niger*), which

can be over 6 m long. It is found in the Amazon and Orinoco Rivers as well as in forest floodplains and swampy lakes. Young caimans have bold, bright colours that become less vivid in adulthood. Prized for its skin, the black caiman is threatened with extinction.

The spectacled caiman (*Caiman crocodilus*) ranges from southern Mexico to northern Argentina. It is hunted more aggressively than the black caiman; half of all skins traded are spectacled caiman skins Smooth-fronted caimans like Schneider's

Florida alligator

North American alligator

smooth-fronted caiman (*Paleosuchus trigonatus*) are less studied and therefore not well understood. Its skin is notably different from that of other caimans, with fewer flexible ridges. Instead, it has bony ossifications that make its skin resemble a turtle's shell.

American alligator

The largest and best-known alligator is the American alligator (*Alligator mississippiensis*) of the south-eastern United States, where it lives in swamps and rivers. American alligators were threatened with extinction primarily through habitat destruction. Wetland habitat conservation laws seek to reverse this process, and alligator populations are currently increasing.

American alligators can be as long as 6 m. They are dark green with irregular dark spots and a light, yellow belly.

A heavy, slow moving animal on land, the American alligator can move with lightning speed in water. It lies in wait for its prey with only its nostrils above the waterline. When an animal comes by, the alligator snaps its jaws and swallows its prey whole or tears it to pieces. Its broad, flat snout can be deceiving. When just below the water, the alligator's smooth snout is somewhat fish-shaped. It can trick victims into thinking the alligator is large fish, like a pike, instead of a deadly predator.

Mating takes place in still water. Males are extremely aggressive during the mating season and frequently engage in violent territorial battles.

Alligator care for the young is very highly developed for a reptile. The male stays with the female for several days after mating while she builds the nest. With powerful movements of her heavy tail, the female alligator shovels mud and plant matter, heaping up the mound into which she will dig a hole and lay her eggs.

An American alligator in Florida. Florida alligators are primarily aquatic. They are well adapted to the environment with their nostrils, eyes and ears all set high on the skull. This allows an alligator to breathe, see and hear with the rest of its body concealed just beneath the water's surface.

Underwater view of an alligator

Young alligators

A female alligator can lay as many as 100 eggs per mating season in her carefully tended nest. She covers the eggs with mud and debris, with the natural compositing of the vegetative matter warming the nest and incubating the eggs. After three weeks the young alligators hatch, calling out to their mother, who opens the nest one last time and lets the now 30-cm long babies out into the sunlight. Young alligators remain near their mother for the first three years of their lives.

Immediately after hatching young alligators hunt for snails and crustaceans, moving on to larger prey like fish, frogs and snakes as they grow. They will not be able to tackle larger prey like birds and large and small mammals until they are full-sized adults.

CHAPTER 6

Testudines

Turtles and tortoises (*Testudines*) are very ancient reptiles. There are over 200 species, most living in tropical and temperate zones. Some live on land, others in the ocean, and many in fresh water.

Turtles and tortoises have a broad abdominal area that is usually entirely enclosed in a shell. The shell consists of a curving upper carapace made of rigid horn plates joined to a flat lower carapace protecting the belly. The upper and lower carapaces are joined together by cartilage that is usually quite soft, although it can be ossified and hard in some species. Although the shell is usually made of horn plates, in some species the hard shell is replaced by leathery skin.

Turtle and tortoise legs, head, neck and tail, covered in flexible scales, can be retracted completely inside the shell if danger threatens. A turtle's head is plump and usually ovoid. Their jaws have no teeth, but, like birds, turtles and tortoises have beaks with horn ridges for cutting and slicing. The neck is extremely flexible.

Most turtles and tortoises are vegetarian, although some terrapins and sea turtles survive on a diet of fish and frogs.

Turtles and tortoises reproduce by laying eggs. Nearly all species lay eggs only on land, even those that are otherwise aquatic. Females dig a hole in the earth or sand, deposit between 10 and 100 roughly spherical eggs, and cover the nest. The eggs hatch within a few weeks or months. After hatching, the young turtles make their way out of the nest into the surrounding area or to the nearest body of water.

Turtles and tortoises are among the animals most threatened with extinction. They and their eggs are eaten as food and their shells are sold for jewelry, as furniture inlays, cosmetic ingredients and traditional medicines. Conservation measures, including breeding programs and import bans, are in place to protect the most endangered species.

Tortoises

Tortoise

There are roughly 40 species of land dwelling tortoises (*Testudinidae*) spread across Europe, Africa, America and Asia. There are no tortoises in Australia.

Tortoises have characteristically clubbed feet and thick, columnar legs. Their toes grow directly from the feet with little articulation. Legs, head and tail are covered with heavy, thick scales. A tortoise shell has a distinct arch, and can be rigid or flexible. Head and limbs can be drawn completely within the shell if danger threatens. When fully retracted, only the very tip of the tail and parts of the forelimbs can be seen. This protective action is necessary because the slow moving

range of patterns. Narrow openings at the front and back of the shell allow the Hermann's tortoise to fully retract its limbs, tail and head.

Tortoises feed on small animals and plants. As pets, they can live on salad, fruit and bread. They have no teeth. All turtles and tortoises slice their food with their beak-like jaws.

Head of a tortoise

tortoises cannot run away from enemies.

Hermann's tortoise (*Testudo hermanni*), most common in southern Europe, is often kept as a pet. Its highly arched upper shell grows to 20–30 cm in length over its flat belly carapace. The upper and lower shells grow together on the sides. Ribs and lumbar vertebrae attach to the inner surface of the shell. The bony surface of the shell has black and yellow horned plates in a wide

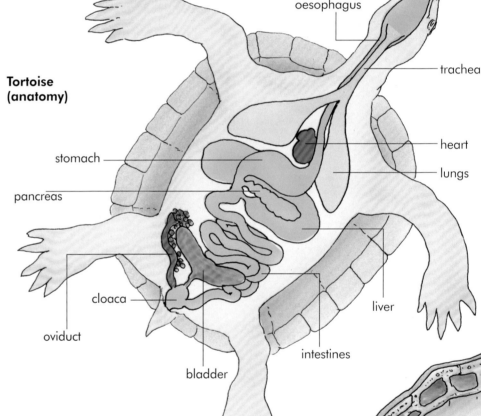

Tortoise (anatomy)

- oesophagus
- trachea
- stomach
- heart
- lungs
- pancreas
- cloaca
- oviduct
- bladder
- liver
- intestines

During the mating season, females look for a sunny area to dig a nest for their walnut-sized eggs. After digging a hole, they lay their eggs and cover the nest over with earth. They then leave, never to return. The heat of the sun will incubate the eggs. After a few months, young turtles just a few centimetres in length hatch.

In temperate climates, tortoises hibernate during the winter in frost-free locations under piles of leaves.

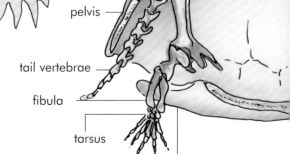

- pelvis
- tail vertebrae
- fibula
- tarsus
- thigh bone (femur)

Other notable tortoises include the hinged tortoise of Africa, which can unhinge part of its shell and drag it behind itself as protection from predators, and the Galapagos tortoise, the largest in the world.

Tortoises play an important role in the mythology of ancient China, where, as one of the five sacred animals, they were believed to be oracles. Their flesh, bile and blood were used to heal a wide variety of illnesses.

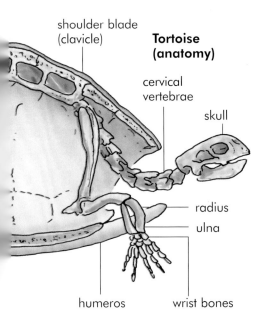

Tortoise (anatomy)

shoulder blade (clavicle)

cervical vertebrae

skull

radius

ulna

humeros

wrist bones

Greek tortoise

The Greek tortoise (*Testudo graeca*) is native to southern Europe, North Africa and the Middle East. It lives in grasslands, forests and farmland. It is one of the best-known species of tortoise.

Its up to 30 cm long shell has a gentle arch. It is yellow with black spots, and therefore superficially with coastal varieties already active again in February. Mating takes place in spring. Males, somewhat smaller than the females, will bite and shove their chosen partner prior to fertilization. Females lay two or three eggs in May or June. These hatch within four months, looking like smaller versions of their parents except for a more articulated shell and overall rounder form.

Greek tortoise (*Testudo graeca*)

very similar to Hermann's tortoise, with which is shares the same geographical range. The Greek tortoise can be identified by the long spurs on the back its rear legs, and by the fact that it does not have a spike at the tip of its tail like Hermann's tortoise does.

The Greek tortoise is primarily vegetarian, but can also eat snails and worms. It hibernates during the winter. It is usually a short sleep,

Greek tortoises are popular pets, although many die due to improper handling. Like most turtles and tortoises, the ease with which they can be captured means their numbers in the wild have greatly declined.

Leopard tortoise

The leopard tortoise (*Geochelone pardalis*) lives in Africa from the Sudan and Ethiopia in the north to South Africa. It prefers dry grassland and open forest habitats.

Leopard tortoises grow to about 60 cm long and weigh some 30 kg.

Leopard tortoise
(*Geochelone pardalis*)

Their shells are particularly interesting. The colour is yellow-brown with irregular black markings that cover the entire shell. Its resemblance to the pelt of a leopard is what gives this tortoise its name. The shape of the turtle is also striking. Its shell has an extraordinarily high arch, with its edges more rectilinear than rounded. Like many tortoises, its rear thighs have horn-like spurs.

The leopard tortoise is vegetarian, living entirely off plants, including fruits and legumes.

Males are aggressive during the mating season, fighting rivals for territory and access to females. Two males will face off head to head, shoving and pushing as each tries to flip the other on its back.

South African female leopard tortoises lay eggs in September and October, but tortoises from warmer climates will extend the mating season even later. Females urinate on the ground to moisten it and then dig a hole with their hind legs. They will deposit between 5 and 30 thick-shelled eggs in the nest. The heavier eggshells protect the embryos both from loss of moisture and from physical damage. Female leopard tortoises may lay eggs several times during each mating season.

Leopard tortoises have the longest incubation period of all turtles and tortoises. It will be more than a year, roughly 450 days, before the young tortoises hatch.

Hinged tortoise

The hinged tortoise (*Kinixys erosa*) is native to West and southern Africa. They live in wet habitats such as swamps, rainforests and alongside rivers. Since they are always near water, they are excellent divers and swimmers. They spend most of their time on land hiding out in shallow pits amid low vegetation.

Hinged tortoises grow to approximately 35 cm in length. They have a uniquely articulated shell that has a hinge between the second and third row of plates. If danger threatens, the shell flops open along the hinge making it difficult for a predator to grab onto the tortoise from the rear. Young tortoises are not born with the hinge; it is only present in adults.

The shell is dark in colour, usually shades of brown or black. The shell plates have a reddish shimmer with a lighter outline. A variant species known as the serrated hinged tortoise has spikes on the front and rear ends of the shell, with the front spiked end extending well in front of the rest of the turtle for extra protection.

Hinged tortoises are exclusively vegetarian. During the mating season, females usually lay about four eggs.

Hinged tortoise (*Kinixys erosa*)

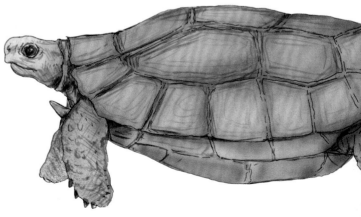

Galapagos tortoise (*Testudo elefantopus*)

Galapagos tortoises

There are two species of giant tortoise in the world, the Seychelles tortoise (*Testudo gigantea*) and the much better known Galapagos tortoise (*Testudo elefantopus*).

The Galapagos tortoise is native to the Galapagos Islands, a volcanic group belonging to the South American country of Ecuador. The islands are famous for their unique ecosystem, which includes a number of animal species found nowhere else in the world. These include six different kinds of giant tortoise, in addition to marine iguanas and a wide variety of birds, fish, seals and sea lions along the coasts.

Galapagos tortoises can grow to 1.2 m in length and weigh 400 kg. They can live more than a century, older than any other animal on earth. The six kinds of Galapagos tortoise vary in the size and shape of their shells. Shell colours are dark brown, green or black.

Many Galapagos tortoises have a bend or outward bowing at the head end of their shells. This gives them the nutritional advantage of being able to raise their heads almost vertically to better reach taller vegetation. Galapagos tortoises also have muscular legs that allow them to easily negotiate the islands' rocky terrain.

Galapagos tortoises have no regular mating season. Males force the much smaller females down to the ground with the front end of their shells until they are in the optimum position for mating. Females dig a pit for their ten or so eggs and then cover them with dirt. The hatchlings must be able to dig their own way out of the nest pit to survive. Galapagos tortoises are fully mature after about twenty years.

Galapagos tortoises love to wallow around in mud. During the dry season, they migrate to the wetter highlands, returning to lower elevations during the rainy season. Like most tortoises, they are vegetarians.

The largest Galapagos tortoises are long extinct. Their preserved shells indicate that they were over 1.70 m long and weighed over a ton. Giant tortoises were hunted nearly to extinction during the nineteenth century. Whalers and pirates landed on these remote islands looking for provisions for long sea journeys. They would capture the tortoises and keep them alive on board, killing them as needed for food along the way.

Over the course of the centuries, it is thought that sailors killed almost 10 million Galapagos tortoises. Conservation programs have ensured that some 10,000 giant tortoises survive on the islands today.

Galapagos tortoises during mating

73

Marsh turtles

Marsh turtles (*Emydidae*) are a diverse group of over 30 genera and 85 species. It is by far the largest of all the turtle and tortoise families. Marsh turtles, closely related to tortoises, are found primarily in the northern hemisphere, with a few isolated species known from Asia and Africa. There are no marsh turtles in Australia. Some marsh turtles are aquatic, living in fresh water environments. Others live in equal measure in water and on land, where they can be seen happily basking in the sun.

The greatest variety of species is native to eastern North America, where they can be divided into three distinct groups. The first are the box turtles (*Terrapene*). They have short heads and particularly wide mouths, and can live on land. Some box turtles are able to shift their shells after retracting their head and limbs so as to close off the openings.

The second group includes true marsh turtles and long-necked

Red-eared slider
(*Crysems scripta*)

Eastern box turtle (*Terrapene caroline caroline*)

Western box turtle (*Terrapene ornata*)

chicken turtles (*Deirochelys*). Both have longer necks and smaller mouths. They are primarily aquatic.

The third group includes the diamond-backed terrapins (*Malaclemys terrapin*) and red-eared sliders (*Chrysems scripta*). These have short necks and wide mouths. They live in brooks and rivers. They are easily identified by the webbing between the toes of their rear limbs, making them much better swimmers than walkers. They are much more at home in water than on land. Their shells are flatter, as if streamlined. When danger threatens, they quickly dive underwater and swim away.

Marsh turtles are omnivorous, eating both plants and animals.

Diamond-backed terrapin

Diamond-backed terrapins (Malaclernys terrapin) are native to the Atlantic and Gulf coasts of the United States. It is the only North American marsh turtle able to tolerate the salt and brackish waters of coastal waters and lagoons. During the day they sit

on sand dunes, wallow in the mud, or wait out the low water in tidal pools. At night they bury themselves deep in the mud.

Diamond-backed terrapins are 15–25 cm long, the males a little smaller than the females. They have powerful rear legs that allow them to move swiftly through the water. They are dark in colour. The upper shell is black, with the horn plates rimmed in red. Each of the horn plates is slightly domed in the centre.

Diamondbacks eat molluscs, worms, snails and young plants.

Mating season is in the spring.

Diamond-backed terrapin
(*malaclemys terrapin*)

Wood turtles

Wood turtles (*Clemmys insculpta*) are native to the deciduous forests of North America. They live largely on land and do not need to be near a body of water except during the mating and hibernation seasons.

Wood turtles grow to about 23 cm. They are robust creatures with a rough-surfaced shell that curves up at the edges. Wood turtles have a flattish head that is usually black in colour. Its neck and limbs are bright orange.

Wood turtles are very intelligent. If they are caught and released somewhere else, they easily find their way back home. They are also good climbers in comparison to other turtles.

During the mating and hibernation seasons, wood turtles migrate to the nearest body of water. Females lay

Wood turtles
(*Clemmys insculpta*)

their eggs in shallow pits on the shore, carefully camouflaging their location with twigs and sand.

Wood turtles live mainly off snails, worms, insects and molluscs, but also eat grass and fruit.

Females dig a nest in a marsh or sand dune, where they lay five to ten eggs. In northern regions the diamond-backed terrapin buries itself in the mud during the autumn and will hibernate until spring.

The flesh of diamond-backed terrapins has long been considered a delicacy. Overhunting has led to the near complete depletion of diamondbacks in many parts of the United States. There are even turtle farms that raise them entirely for their meat.

Spotted turtle

The spotted turtle (*Clemmys guttata*) is native to the north-east of the United States and nearby parts of Canada. They are primarily aquatic, living on the banks of old quarries and in small ponds.

The spotted turtle is one of the smallest of all freshwater turtles at just 10–13 cm long. Males and females are the same size, and both have belly shells that are slightly concave. Spotted turtles have blue-black shells covered in bright yellow teardrop-shaped spots. The number of spots is directly related to the age of the turtle. The older a spotted turtle is, the greater the number of spots. In old age, the colour of the spots becomes noticeably less intense.

Spotted turtles eat worms, snails, insects and plants. After mating, females lay 3–12 eggs in a shallow pit. If threatened, the otherwise defenceless spotted turtles retract

Spotted turtle (*Clemmys guttata*)

their head and limbs inside their shells. They also dive into the water and dig into the mud. In the winter, they dig hibernation dens in the mud and stay there until spring.

Spotted turtles can live to be forty years or more.

75

Sea turtles

Sea turtles live in warm and temperate saltwater aquatic habitats like oceans and bays. They were once land tortoises that returned to the sea some 150 million years ago.

Sea turtles have adapted to their maritime environment so well that they are now very different from tortoises and marsh turtles. They have much flatter shells streamlined for swimming, and their forelimbs are flat and paddle-like. They use these two powerful limbs to literally "fly" through the water at impressive speeds and for very long distances. Each limb has one or two vestigial claws. The rear limbs are much shorter than the forelimbs and primarily help with steering. A major difference between sea turtles and other kinds of turtles and tortoises is that sea turtles cannot retract their head or limbs under their shells.

Sea turtles eat snails, jellyfish and molluscs, but also algae and sea grass. They spend nearly their entire lives in water. After mating, the female must crawl up on the sand to lay her eggs, using her flat limbs to dig out a pit, usually in the dead of night. She covers the eggs with sand and crawls back into the water.

Sea turtle eggs hatch after two or three months. They must also crawl back to the water, a dangerous journey that only a very small percentage of baby turtles complete. Even fewer will survive to adulthood. Those that make it through the early years can live fifty years or more.

There are two families of sea turtles. The Cheloniidae include the green sea turtle, hawskbill sea turtle, false hawksbill, flatback sea turtle, Ridley sea turtles and Kemp's Ridley sea turtles.

Loggerhead sea turtle
(*Caretta caretta*)

Green sea turtle

The green sea turtle (*Chelonia mydas*) lives in all the oceans of the world in waters where the temperature constantly remains above 20 °C. They are common in coastal waters, but can also be found on the high seas.

Green sea turtles grow up to 1.3 m long and have a brownish-red shell. Their horn plates have lighter coloured rim. Males have a somewhat longer, narrower shell than females and large, curved claws on their forelimbs. They use these to firmly grasp females during mating. Green sea turtles are primarily vegetarian, but occasionally eat jellyfish and small crustaceans.

Every two or three years, male and female green turtles return to the same nesting site on a sandy beach, always returning to the place where they themselves hatched. This is often hundreds of miles away from their feeding grounds as adults. After mating, the female pulls herself out of the water. Once on land, sea turtles are very ungainly beasts, dragging themselves forward on their flat, paddle feet until they are beyond the reach of the tides. The female digs a shallow pit with her forelimbs and sits inside it. She then digs a deeper pit

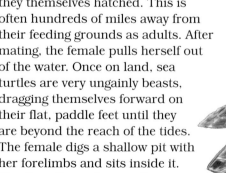

themselves out of the sand. They immediately turn toward the sea. On their way to the water, many young sea turtles will fall victim to predators. Those that make it to the ocean encounter more dangers there.

The green sea turtle is nearly extinct in many parts of the world and is only rarely sighted today. It was long hunted for its skin, shell and meat. Hunters would wait for the nearly defenceless turtles on the nesting beaches, where they were easy to capture. Since then, hunting sea turtles is banned in most countries, as is the import of any sea turtle products.

Northern Australia is home to the green sea turtle's close relative, the flatback turtle (*Chelonia depressa*). It spends all its time in coastal waters. Flatback turtles are smaller than their green sea turtle cousins.

Green sea turtle
(*Chelonia mydas*)

directly under her tail, this time digging with her hind limbs.

The pit is around 40 cm deep and may hold up to 100 eggs. Once the female has laid her eggs, she crawls back into the sea. A female green turtle may lay eggs more than once during the mating season in two-week increments. The young turtles hatch in two or three months, digging

Hawskbill sea turtles

True hawksbill sea turtles (*Eretmochelys imbracata*) live in the tropical regions of the Atlantic, Pacific and Indian Oceans, as well as in the Caribbean Sea. Their preferred habitats are rocky coastlines and coral reefs.

True hawksbills are 75–90 cm long with light-coloured shells covered in a mosaic-like pattern of reddish brown markings. Its horn plates are exceptionally strong. The edges of the shell are serrated for extra protection. Hawksbill sea turtles get their name from their long, pointed

snout that terminates in a horn beak. They use it to pull small crustaceans and other invertebrates from between rocks and reefs.

Hawksbill sea turtles do not have to journey as far as other sea turtles in order to reproduce. Their feeding grounds are always near a coast. Females crawl on land and lay up to 150 eggs at a time. No other turtle lays so many eggs.

Hawksbill sea turtles were hunted primarily for their magnificent mosaic shells. Both hunting hawksbill turtles and importing their shells are now banned in most countries.

True hawskbill turtle
(*Eretmochelys imbracata*)

Leatherback sea turtles

The leatherback sea turtle (*Dermochelys coriacea*) is the largest aquatic turtle in the world. It can live in any warm sea. They can grow to 2.5 m long and weigh between 350 and 600 kg. This makes it the largest turtle of all, bigger than the largest Galapagos tortoise. With its fin-like forelimbs fully extended, its full span is nearly 2.7 m. Its shell is somewhat elongated, rather than rounded, and thinner at the ends. It consists of seven domed linear sections, usually dark grey or black and slightly lighter in colour down the middle. Light coloured spots cover both upper and lower shell. The shell itself is made of bone rather than the horn plates most turtles have. The leatherback sea turtle shell is really a thick, oily, leathery skin, comparable in density and strength to anodized rubber. Both the shell and the rest of the leatherback's skin lack the keratinized scales of other reptiles. The leatherback sea turtle's diet consists nearly entirely of jellyfish.

Every two years, leatherback sea turtles make the long journey back to their nesting beach, where they will mate in the coastal waters. The female laboriously crawls through the sand to lay her eggs. When she is a safe distance from the water, she digs a hole with her hind limbs and deposits 80–100 eggs, covering them over carefully with sand. The female leatherback then circles the nest once more before heading back to the sea. During the mating season, females will lay a clutch of eggs every ten days.

The newly hatched leatherbacks, just 6 cm long, dig themselves out of the sand and head instinctively toward water. Young turtles have scales instead of the leathery shell, which will develop over time as they grow into adults.

Head of a snapping turtle
(*Chelydra serpentina*)

Leatherback sea turtle
(*Dermochelys coriacea*)

Snapping turtle

The snapping turtle (Chelydra serpentina) is common throughout the Americas. These aggressive, biting reptiles have powerful jaws similar to those of a crocodile. They spend most of their time buried in the mud beneath still bodies of water.

Other turtles and tortoises

There are many other fascinating species of turtle that, although similar in many ways, have evolved differently in response to variations in environment.

Fly River turtle

The Fly River turtle (*Carettochelys insculpta*), known in the pet trade as the pig-nosed turtle, lives in the rivers and brackish waters of Papua New Guinea. Considered one of the more primitive varieties of turtle, this soft-shelled species is one of the last remaining fresh water turtles with a full bony shell covered with leathery skin instead of horn plates. Its distinctive nose resembles a pig's snout.

Head of a Fly River *(pig-nosed)* turtle *(Carettochelys insculpta)*

Head of a true soft-shelled turtle

True soft-shell turtle

The true soft-shell turtle (*Trionychinae*) is native to the fresh water habitats of Africa, North America and Asia. They are excellent divers that can stay submerged for hours due to a set of gills that supplements their air-breathing lungs.

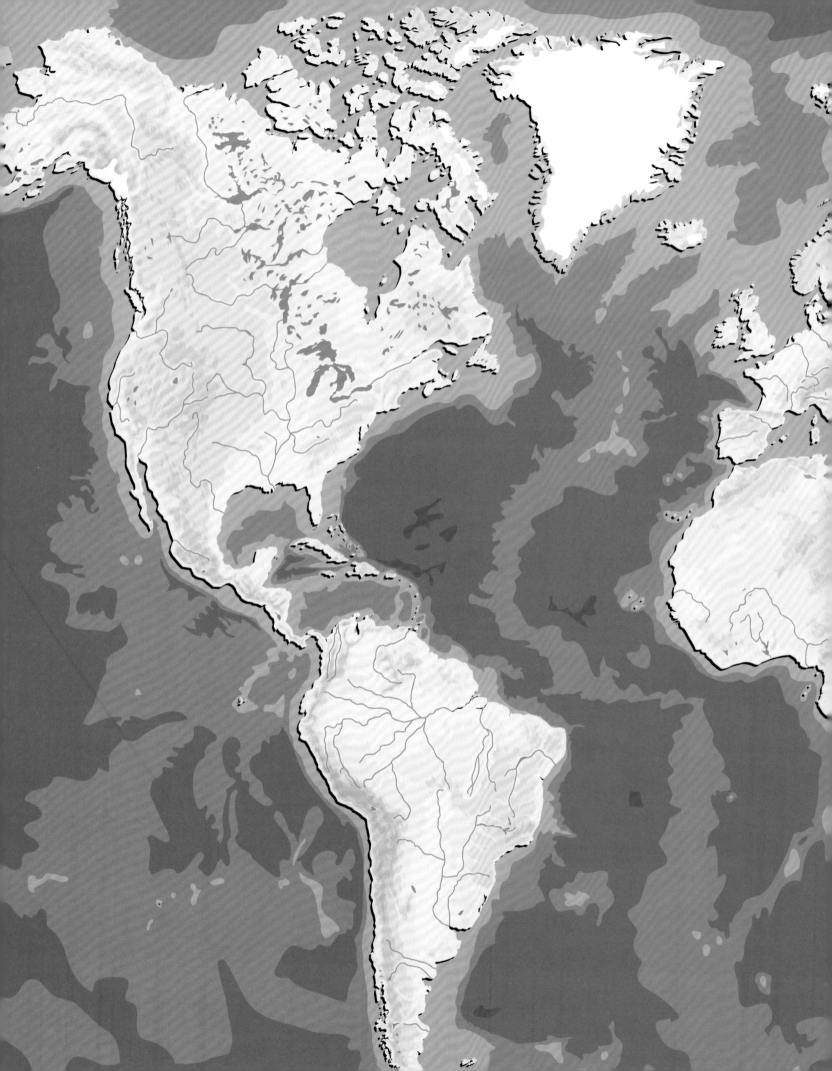

Habitats

The earth's species are distributed over a range of climate and vegetation zones. Each species is adapted to its local conditions and can tolerate only limited variation in climatic conditions. Most amphibians and reptiles will die off if they are forced out of their environment. In addition to adequate rainfall and temperature, a sustainable environment must provide adequate food and protection against predators.

Topographical features also limit a species' range. For land animals, large bodies of water or high mountain ranges are effective boundaries. This is why islands like Madagascar are home to animals that are very different from those on the African mainland.

The animal kingdom can also be separated into terrestrial and aquatic species. Terrestrial animals live on land and can be found everywhere, from the poles and tundra to mixed and deciduous forests. Other land environments include grasslands, among them the African savannah, South American pampas, North American prairie, and steppes of Europe and Asia. The tropical rainforest is a particularly rich ecosystem found on either side of the equator. Mountain environments are also home to animal populations that change as the elevation increases.

Aquatic animals are divided into freshwater and saltwater species. Freshwater animals are further subdivided into those that prefer rushing water, like that of rivers, brooks and streams, and those that can only live and breed where the waters are still, such as lakes, swamps and ponds. Most rivers run to the sea. In contrast to still waters, rivers have strong currents, flow in one direction and have a higher oxygen content.

Deciduous forest

Blindworm
(*Anguis fragilis*),
Africa, Asia and Europe

Broad-headed skink
(*Eumeces laticeps*)

In an evolutionary sense, widespread deciduous forests are relatively recent. Today they are found in central Europe, eastern North America and East Asia.

All deciduous forests on earth date back just 10,000 years to the last glacial retreat. Species that survived the ice age in warmer regions migrated into the newly temperate zones. In North America and East Asia, topographical boundaries to species expansion were few. In Europe, however, the Alps were a substantial barrier. As a result, compared to similar environments elsewhere, the European deciduous forest has a more limited variety of plant and animals species.

Deciduous forest habitats are defined by clear seasons. Winter halts most animal and plant activity for several months. Plants and animals survive by a variety of means. Deciduous trees slow their metabolism by shedding their leaves, while other dormant plants live off energy stored in bulbs, seeds and tubers. Birds can escape winter's cold and limited food by migrating to a warmer region. Many amphibians, reptiles and insects hibernate, as do many mammals. Other animals survive the winter months by collecting food the rest of the year.

The once extensive, continuous deciduous forest has been decimated by human agriculture over the past two millennia. Recent research shows that every forest goes through a variety of stages. Open land becomes home to trees that grow into a mature forest. After hundreds of years, these stands of mature trees become old growth

Scandinavia

North America
USA
Mexico

Europe

Africa

South America

Deciduous forest

forests. As trees begin to fall down, they create a rich array of microenvironments, especially beech forests.

An old growth forest ends up as a mixture of forest and clearings. A forest clearing goes through phases each year. In spring, before the trees have leaves, a clearing receives a lot of sunlight. The plants that grow in spring are therefore different than those that grow in the summer, when a clearing will be heavily shaded. In winter, it is too cold for anything to grow.

The snow cover protects most of the organisms living in the soil from

freezing to death. The heavy leaf litter layer found in forests is a major source of protection and nutrition for decomposers like bacteria, worms and fungi.

The warmer the climate, the more likely it is that the flora keep their leaves all year round. Forests dominated by laurel, eucalyptus and asters fit this profile. Within the temperate deciduous zone, evergreen forests like these are relatively rare and limited in area. Individual stretches of deciduous forest can exhibit a high degree of biodiversity with their own unique species of trees, plants and animals. Many of these unique environments no longer exist due to a long history of human depredation and clearing for agriculture.

Wood turtle
(*Clemmys insculpta*), eastern North America

Amphibian and reptile species in deciduous forests

The cold winters common to deciduous forests mean that reptiles and amphibians are only able to forage for food during the warm months of the year. Most are already going into hibernation in early autumn, burying themselves under the thick layer of fallen leaves, in burrows dug into the forest floor or in the muddy bottoms of ponds. Both reptiles and amphibians need to live near water all year round, which necessarily limits the number of species that can survive in the forest.

Fire salamanders are a typical forest amphibian species. Forest and rock lizards prefer to live on the fringes of the forest because they need open space to sun themselves during the day. They also live off insects that also need the warmth of the sun to survive.

Blindworms and grass snakes are forest reptiles that need to stay moist. While the blindworm can manage this on the forest floor, the grass snake is more commonly spotted in or near water. The European viper is venomous, but shy. It prefers dry habitats, but can also be found in moorland.

Toads are amphibians that do very well on the forest floor. They are primarily terrestrial and adapt easily to a wide variety of conditions.

Turtles and tortoises are entirely absent from the forests of central Europe, but a number of diverse species are common in North America. Box turtles are terrestrial marsh turtles well adapted to forest life, as are the eastern diamondback and mosaic turtles. Tortoises are well represented in the deciduous forests of Southeast Asia.

Among reptiles, the false monitor and whiptail lizard are also found in North American forests, while Southeast Asian forests are rich in skink species, which migrate into deciduous regions from warmer zones.

Tropical rainforest

Rainbow agama (agama agama), central Africa

The term "tropical rainforest" is often synonymous in popular imagination with the jungle and the lush environment it evokes. While it is true that the rainforest is home to a greater variety of plants than anywhere else on earth, the word actually stems from the Indian "jangal", describing a south-east Asian environment notable for its rough, waterless terrain.

It is not easy to spot animals in rainforest, and visitors are often disappointed that there are so few animals to be seen. There are very few large animals in the rainforest, and it is nearly impossible to see the well-camouflaged smaller inhabitants through the thick canopy of leaves. Insects are by far the most common, followed by amphibians and reptiles. Birds and mammals tend to be solitary or travel in pairs, living far from other members of their species.

In one well-documented rainforest in Costa Rica, there were more than 100 species of mammal, 400 birds, 50 reptiles and 41 amphibians, but over 4000 species of butterfly. In another famous study, more than 43 species of ant were found inhabiting a single tree. More than 3000 kinds of beetle were counted in the canopies of just five trees.

Scientists debate whether there are 2 million or 30 milion species of rainforest plants and animals. A complete, systematic study of rainforests around the world has yet to take place. That rainforests are among the more species-rich environments is undisputed.

The range of individual rainforest species is highly restricted; rainfor-

Green mamba (Dendroaspis viridis), West Africa

North America
USA
Mexico
Central America
South America
Brazil
Europe
Africa
Mad
Antarctica

Rainforest with wet and dry seasons

Rainforest without wet and dry seasons

est plants and animals rarely survive outside their own unique habitats. Even if the neighbouring habitat seems similar, the adaptations of each species are very precise. They have had a lot of time to evolve in very specific ways. Every niche within a rainforest is already occupied, making immigration by a new species difficult.

If humans had not cut down so many trees for agriculture, there would probably be about 17 million square km (nearly 12% of the earth's surface) of rainforest. But by 1980 more than a third had been

destroyed. As much as 10% of the remaining rainforest is cut down every year. The largest continuous rainforests left are in the Amazon basin, south-east Asia and Africa.

In the rainforest, the growth cycle of plants and animals is uninterrupted all round. They have an average temperature of 25–27 °C and an average rainfall of 2000–3000 mm per year. There are no seasons, just cooler nights and warmer days.

The rainforest is also, oddly, a nutritional wasteland, where the soils are nearly devoid of nutrients. The rainforest survives because the

Carpet python
(*Morelia spilota*), Australia
and Papua New Guinea

very limited nutrients are constantly cycled and recycled through the plants and animals that live there.

Most rainforest animals live in the forest canopy more than 50 m above the forest floor. The climate is more amenable, and the main source of nutrition, leaves, are readily available because there is more light higher up. There are also parasitic plants (Epiphyten) that live in the canopy branches of host trees without ever coming in contact with the ground. They collect water in funnel-like leaves, in the process creating a habitat for small aquatic creatures.

At the most, just 1% of the available sunlight reaches the forest floor. As a result, almost no leafy vegetation can grow there. Plants only cover the forest floor in clearings and along the banks of rivers.

Mangrove forests are a very specific variety of rainforest that grows only in very wet, flooded locations. Mangrove trees have uniquely adapted by evolving roots that take in nutrients through the air while providing secure anchorage in unstable mud. Terrestrial animals cannot survive in a Mangrove swamp, but aquatic life forms, such as amphibians, thrive there.

Amphibian and reptile species in the rainforest

Reptiles love the moist heat of the rainforest. Their environment-dependent body temperature gives them an advantage over warm-blooded mammals and birds. Amphibians benefit from the rainforest's sheer amount of rainfall and the ample standing water that results.

Amphibians occupy more than just the ponds and rivers that run through the forest. They also live in the tree canopy. Rainwater collects in the funnel-shaped parasitic plants

(*Ephiphyten*), creating mini pools of water. The amphibians that live there are miniature, like their environment. Most are tiny aquatic frogs.

Since climbing through the canopy requires a good grip, the reptiles that live there have evolved complex mechanisms for climbing, including claws and adhesive pads for gripping and special scales on their tails to help them hang on. Rainforest native tree snakes, rainbow agamas, iguanas and monitor lizards all have these.

Other reptiles have evolved skin flaps that help them glide from branch to branch or tree to tree. The flying dragon is a 12-cm long agama from Indonesia. It has skin hanging from its rib cage that can be extended between its four limbs. When fully extended, a flying dragon can easily glide over distances up to 15 m.

Snakes are also expert canopy jumpers and gliders. The brightly coloured ones use their colouration to send out a warning that they are venomous. The most venomous snakes in the world are the African mambas. The 2-m long green mamba waits in tree branches for its prey, mainly lizards and birds. The black mamba, nearly twice as long, prefers to stay on the ground, as is the case for nearly all giant snakes. The boas in South and Central America and pythons of Africa, Asia and Australia are all rainforest natives. Both boas and pythons grasp their prey firmly with their teeth, then wrap around their victims, strangling them before devouring them.

The largest venomous snake in the Americas is the bushmaster, at 3.5 m long. Like all inhabitants of the rainforest floor, it prefers a moist environment. The Gabon viper of Africa is another ground dweller.

Steppe and savannah

Both savannah and steppe undergo extreme rainfall and temperature changes throughout the year, transforming the living conditions for plants and animals from one season to the next. The most significant factor is the dry season that causes severe water shortages.

While most steppe and savannah environments undergo an annual transformation between wet and dry season, the temperature transition between summer and winter can also be extreme, particularly in combination with seasonal precipitation patterns.

The African savannah's rainy season is related to its proximity to rainforest latitudes. The near constant rain clouds above the rainforests shift between 10 degrees north and 10 degrees south of the equator depending on the angle of sun. The savannah lies on the edges of this zone, receiving heavy rains only once or twice each year. The rest of the time, it is dry. This near-desert environment averages just 600 mm of rain per year.

Although the African savannah is the best known, India, Australia and South America (the Pantanal) also have extensive savannahs.

Savannahs are grasslands with occasional stands of drought-tolerant trees and shrubs. The grasses create a dense network of surface roots that absorb the majority of rainy season precipitation. With the rains come tender new shoots providing a rich source of nutrition for numerous animals. In the dry season, only the rootstock survives.

Savannah trees often retain their leaves all year round due to drought adaptations that include special organs for storing water.

There are variations of the savannah in Africa that are actually quite wet. In areas with topographical depressions, water collects and soaks the surrounding terrain until it is more properly described as moorland. Palm trees and tall savannah grasses like elephant grass, which can be 6 m high, are found there, often on forest land previously cleared for cultivation.

Steppes are dry grassland environments usually in the interior of continents. They are drier than African grasslands, with approximately 400 mm of rain per year. Winters are typically severe with an early hard frost and constant strong winds. No trees grow here except along the banks of rivers and streams. As in the savannah, the upper layer of soil is made of grass roots. Lacking drought-tolerant trees, herbaceous plants with taproots for water conservation are the only large plant that can grow there.

Canada

North America
USA
Mexico

Central America

South America

Europe

Africa

South Africa

Antarctic

Savannah/pampas

Prairie/steppe

At the highest elevations, there is less oxygen in the air. In addition, the lack of cloud cover at increases the amount of UV-radiation.

Animals of the high mountain ranges vary with altitude much like the plant world. The Rocky Mountains and Alps are home to populations of animals similar or identical to those in northern tundra environments as well at to other species that have evolved to live only on specific mountains within a specific vegetation zone.

Amphibians and reptiles in the mountains

The colder the climate, the harder it is for cold-blooded animals to survive. Despite this, mountain ranges are home to a variety of amphibians and reptiles.

One of these is the alpine salamander, which has been identified at elevations as high as 3000 m. The alpine salamander is the rare amphibian that is nearly entirely terrestrial. Three years or so after mating, females give birth to live young with fully developed lungs. This long period of development is related to the long winters and the time the female has to spend in hibernation.

Another record holder among mountain amphibians is an Andean frog that lives at elevations up to 4000 m, and the Himalaya skink spotted at 5000 m.

Other mountain amphibians and reptiles include the mountain newt, grass frog, mountain lizard and European viper.

Amphibians and reptiles that are highly adapted to cave environments are also common in the mountains, although not all caves are at high altitudes. The blind cave salamander is one of these. The moist environment with, constant, regular temperature is ideal for these salamanders.

much like the surrounding temperature latitudes. During winter many animals migrate down the mountain to warmer valleys.

Lakes and rivers

A wide variety of animals and plants live around lakes and rivers. All have adapted to life in or near water. They may be entirely aquatic, while others

Nile crocodile (*Crocodylus niloticus*), Africa, with the exception of the Sahara and northwest Africa

live part of the time on land, part of the time in water. Some may have lungs, others breathe with gills.

Lakes and rivers offer a range of environmental conditions as well. Lakes have less oxygen than rivers. Lake water is not churned by currents like river water, and therefore has layers and levels where different temperature and other abiotic factors define environmental conditions. The upper layer of a lake in winter may be solid ice, but further down, it is warmer. During the summer, these temperature and depth relationships are reversed. In temperate zones, spring and autumn convection currents cause the warm and cold levels to mix. In tropical lakes, no part of the lake will fall below 4 °C. There is little temperature stratification, but certain zones of the lake will have higher or lower levels of nutrients and oxygen.

The bottom of a lake is typically the level with the least oxygen despite the fact that this is where oxygen is most needed to break down the dead organisms that sink down through the water. The lack of oxygen and sunlight means that no plants grow at the bottom of a lake.

The rushing water of a river is constantly churned by currents and therefore better mixed. As a river reaches the sea, the current slows and the riverbed becomes muddy with accumulated silt. The water temperature rises, but variations in temperature and nutrients become more extreme.

Individual European rivers are typically divided into different sections named after their dominant fish species. Waters near the source European rivers are called the trout zone, followed by the greyling and barbel zones, and ending with the carp zone near the river mouth.

The quality of the nutritional material and silt that a river carries is dependent on the kind of bedrock and organic material it encounters along the way.

Canada

North America
USA
Mexico

Central America

South America

Europe

Africa

Lakes and rivers

Bullfrog (Rana catesbeiana), eastern North America

animals live side by side in these places depending on their tolerance for cyclical flooding and drought. Several species have evolved with adaptations to survive the constant shift between wet and dry. As a result, many river and stream valleys are unique ecosystems.

There are also lakes and swamps that exist only after heavy seasonal rains flood an otherwise dry region. Here, too, species are adapted to survive the annual extremes of drought before the life-giving rains return.

Amphibians and reptiles in rivers and lakes

Crocodiles evolved well before the dinosaur era. All predators, the sharp teeth of these large reptiles snap down on their prey in less than a second. Even humans have to take care when crocodiles and alligators are around. Crocodiles and alligators spend most of their time lolling around in the water, often just below the surface. True crocodiles live only in tropical zones, but alligators and caimans can range into subtropical climates in America. Gavials are native to Southeast Asia.

Many snakes are aquatic. Their terrestrial locomotion style works equally well when swimming through water. One of the largest snakes in the world, the South American anaconda, lies on the bottom of shallow lakes and wetlands waiting for prey. The checkered keelback is a large snake native to the Indonesian island of Java. It rarely leaves the water. Water moccasins lead an amphibious life in and out of ponds and swamps, hunting a wide variety of animals.

Turtles and tortoises are only rarely fully aquatic. Many spend more time on land than in water. Marsh turtles, however, tend to prefer the water, leaving it only to sun themselves on the banks of rivers,

ponds and streams. The Southeast Asian big head turtle lives off water snails that it catches in mountain streams. The enormous alligator snapping turtle of North and South America, which has a shell that grows over 1 m in length, lies on the bottom of lakes and streams waiting for its prey. Soft shell turtles native to the northern hemisphere are so well adapted to the aquatic environment that they have webbing between their toes. The freshwater habitats of the southern hemisphere are home to the aquatic snake-necked and medusa turtles.

Newts are a kind of salamander widely distributed throughout the northern hemisphere. Most spend their larval stage in water, which is also where they return to mate. The rest of their lives are spent in thick vegetation along the banks.

Frogs and toads are found all around the world with the exception of very dry or very cold regions. Frog larvae, or tadpoles, are fully aquatic, while adults are usually primarily terrestrial. The European water frog and yellow-bellied toad are two species that never stray far from water. There are also tongueless frogs native to tropical zones in South America and Africa that never leave the water. Lacking tongues, frogs in this use their long digits to dig for food in the muddy lake and river bottoms.

The fastest developing of all frogs and toads are the spadefoots, a primitive species whose tadpoles hatch after two days and are fully metamorphosed into adults within 12 days. They are well adapted to the extreme wet and dry conditions, burying themselves in the hot desert sand, where they wait for the heavy rains of the rainy season. Although spadefoots are technically desert creatures, they flourish during the brief periods when their environment is underwater. If the rains don't come, spadefoot eggs can survive for years without hatching.

Rivers that travel through tropical rainforests are black with humic acid from the massive decay of organic material along their banks, but lack nutrients because the soils washed into rivers are nutrient poor. In contrast, a pond surrounded by cultivated fields will be brown in colour and rich in nutrients from fertilizer and manure runoff.

River valleys are technically terrestrial habitats, but are often in between aquatic and terrestrial because they are regularly flooded. Water and land

INDEX